Ubud
The Spirit of Bali

Ubud
The Spirit of Bali

Hermawan Kartajaya
Bembi Dwi Indrio M.

PT Gramedia Pustaka Utama, Jakarta

Ubud
The Spirit of Bali
Copyright © 2009 by PT Gramedia Pustaka Utama

This English edition is published by PT Gramedia Pustaka Utama
Kompas Gramedia Building, Tower I, 4th–5th Fl.
Jl. Palmerah Barat 29–37, Jakarta 10270
Member of IKAPI, Jakarta 2009

GM 204 01 09 0125

Authors: Hermawan Kartajaya with Bembi Dwi Indrio M.
Cover design: Renny S. Wijaya
English translation: Ted Thornton
Layout: Adhitya Dharma

Unless otherwise credited, all images are taken by and copyright of Bembi
Dwi Indrio M.

ISBN: 978-979-22-4987-3

Printed by PT Gramedia Printing, Jakarta

Table of Content

Prologue

Ubud: The Spirit of Bali

Om Swastiastu. May Almighty God bless you all.

Over the past few years, the writers of this book have regularly visited Ubud, on the island of Bali. Ubud has a unique appeal that keeps us coming back; we're never bored there. And we have also become close to Ubud's royal family, particularly Drs. Tjokorda Gde Raka Sukawati MM, or Tjok 'De, one of the sons of the last King of Ubud.

Though we rarely stay very long—typically just two or three days—we always thoroughly enjoy these brief visits, which seem to quickly erase all the stress that has accumulated from our daily work routine. And when we return to Jakarta, we feel reborn; our spirits are restored; our mood is happier and more relaxed. And we believe that most people who have visited Ubud feel the same way.

So we began to wonder: What is it about Ubud? What makes us, and so many others, fall in love with this place? Why do people keep coming back to Ubud, or even decide to live there?

Upon reflection, we came to realize that the attraction of Ubud lies not only in its tangible aspects—what is evident to the naked eye—but also in the intangible side. Together, the tangible and the intangible worlds create what is known in Hindu-Bali culture as *taksu*, which can be translated roughly as "spiritual charm".

It is this *taksu* that makes Ubud so different from other places. *Taksu* is the "vibe" that transforms a person, making us feel new again.

This *taksu* has not just appeared out of nowhere. It has developed because the society of Ubud follows a three-way philosophy of life called "*Tri Hita Karana*": harmonious relations between humans and God, between humans and the natural environment, and among humans. This philosophy is fundamental to all activities that take place in Ubud. *Tri Hita Karana* has been applied consistently in daily life for centuries; this is how Ubud's *taksu* has come about.

Ubud's stunning natural panoramas, its friendly, spiritual people who firmly uphold their traditional culture, and the many incomparable art works—paintings, wood carvings, dance performances, and even culinary arts—all of these contribute to Ubud's intense *taksu*. So many things, both visible (known to the Hindu-Balinese as *skala*) and invisible (known as *niskala*), make us increasingly aware of the purpose and meaning of our existence as humans in this world.

What's more, Ubud provides these benefits not only to individuals; in a broader perspective, Ubud, and the way it has been managed, offers inspiration for the world of business.

How so?

Recently, we've witnessed the collapse of many major corporations, especially in the United States and Europe. These companies suffered tremendous financial losses and consequently had to take drastic steps they had never before contemplated. Some companies had to lay off many of their employees; others were forced to accept buyout bids from competitors, or to receive government bailouts; and quite a few simply went bankrupt.

These conditions have since spread to all parts of the world. Nearly all leading global companies have been affected one way or another. Many say that this current financial and economic crisis is on the same scale as the Great Depression of the 1930s. All this clearly indicates that there have been some fundamental problems with the way business has been conducted.

If we look more closely, we see that the symptoms were already evident at the start of this century, in the financial manipulations of Enron and other similar cases that followed. But businesses failed to draw the appropriate lessons from these failures. The subprime mortgage crisis swept through the United States economy in 2007, and then triggered a whole series of crises in the business world, which are still continuing.

At around the same time, the world began to suffer a food crisis. Food prices skyrocketed, leading to political, economic and social instability in many countries. Many factors were blamed: prolonged droughts in some parts of the world, steadily rising population levels, and the actions of speculators in the food commodity markets.

The world has also experienced serious problems from sharp fluctuation in crude oil prices. The continuing heavy dependence on oil as a major energy source has made it difficult for many industries to formulate business plans, since fuel prices have been so unpredictable. End consumers have also suffered from sudden surges in fuel prices or even shortages of fuel for their vehicles.

Another very serious problem currently faced by the world community is global warming and climate change. The steadily rising temperature on this planet has led to drastic changes in climate patterns. Tropical storms have become more intense and more frequent; floods have struck regions where they never occurred before; all over the world, the weather is getting noticeably hotter. All this indicates that the balance of nature is being disturbed, and the earth is becoming a less hospitable place for human life.

These problems—food, fuel, finance, and climate change—will obviously cause drastic changes in the business landscape.

But why did all this happen? What went wrong?

In our view, all these problems occurred because of business practices that ignored basic values. Moral hazards arose everywhere, because so many business operators were blinded by the prospect of generating maximum profits, no matter what the costs to others or to the planet; they neglected spiritual, social and environmental values. This narrow, short-term outlook backfired: it not only ruined their businesses but also had a huge negative impact on humankind and on the environment as a whole.

Based on this, for the past four or five years we have been promoting the idea that sound business practices and positive values are actually inseparable. And since we feel that the foundation of business is marketing, marketing practices can no longer ignore the values prevailing in the community where the marketing is being done.

As we see it, there are three basic patterns in the relationship between marketing and values. The first is *polarization*: an absolute separation between marketing and values. This polarization derives from an attitude that applying values to marketing will only increase costs, and is therefore unnecessary.

The second pattern is *balancing*. In this approach, it is considered acceptable if marketing practices violate or deviate from ethical standards, as long as some of the profits are later donated to social welfare activities, in a kind of trade-off.

The third pattern is *integration*. In this approach, marketing and values are no longer seen as separate; marketing and values are unified, and each reinforces the other. This is clearly the best of these three approaches, as it is both the most advantageous for all concerned and the most sustainable in the long term.

Therefore, companies and institutions can no longer apply the polarized or balancing approaches to the relationship between marketing and values; integration is essential for success.

Seen from another perspective, there have also been shifts in marketing approaches. In the past, marketers simply tried to offer their existing products or services, with little concern for whether these products were actually what customers needed. This was the *product-centric* era.

Later, as they came to recognize that the most important thing is the customer, rather than the product itself, marketers began to study customers' desires, needs and expectations before they even developed new products. This was what we call the *customer-centric* era of marketing.

But then, with the many changes in the business landscape, and particularly changes in the behavior and psychology of customers, the customer-centric approach was no longer considered adequate. Customers want to be treated as whole human beings, not just as pawns in the marketing game. It was recognized that they have deep anxieties and desires, in addition to their traditional needs and wants. Customers want greater participation in the creation of values aimed at them. This is the *human-centric* era.

If we call the product-centric era Marketing 1.0, and the customer-centric era Marketing 2.0, then the human-centric era is Marketing 3.0.[1]

We can see that the integration of marketing and values matches perfectly with Marketing 3.0, because only people with proper values can survive in the current world of business. In this concept, marketing is fully integrated with profit-making and social responsibility. The emphasis is not solely on seeking profits; everything is integrated, and therefore more sustainable as well. This model of marketing can provide solutions to the many problems the world currently faces.

And we are not alone in thinking this. Many other experts have expressed similar ideas and visions.

At the individual level, books such as *The 8th Habit: From Effectiveness to Greatness* by Stephen R. Covey or *Spiritual Capital: Wealth We Can Live By* by Danah Zohar and Ian Marshall show the importance of the spiritual aspect in each individual's personal development.

At the organizational level, many experts have raised the importance of awareness of green issues in business management. These include Thomas L. Friedman in *Hot, Flat, and Crowded: Why We Need a Green*

Revolution—and How It Can Renew America; Peter M. Senge in *The Necessary Revolution: How Individuals and Organizations Are Working Together to Create a Sustainable World*; and Daniel Goleman in *Ecological Intelligence: How Knowing the Hidden Impacts of What We Buy Can Change Everything*. And we mustn't forget the book and the Oscar-winning documentary film by Al Gore, *An Inconvenient Truth*.

Other literature focuses on how caring about society can ensure sustainable business practices. This issue is discussed by writers such as C.K. Prahalad in his book *The Fortune at the Bottom of the Pyramid: Eradicating Poverty through Profits*; Jeffrey D. Sachs in *Common Wealth: Economics for a Crowded Planet*; John Elkington and Pamela Hartigan in *The Power of Unreasonable People: How Social Entrepreneurs Create Markets That Change the World*; and Stuart L. Hart in *Capitalism at the Crossroads: Aligning Business, Earth, and Humanity*.

Another important example of community empowerment is the ideas and the work of Prof. Muhammad Yunus and the Grameen Bank, which won the Nobel Peace Prize in 2006.

So how does all this relate to Ubud?

For us, Ubud is the most genuine and complete manifestation of Marketing 3.0, representing a full integration of marketing and values.

Why?

Because Ubud doesn't simply offer the "product" that it already has (Marketing 1.0), or try to create a "product" needed by its customers (Marketing 2.0); rather, it markets "products" that can transform people (Marketing 3.0). And this is possible because Ubud has long been managed with a view to the integration of marketing and values.

As a tourism destination, it's fair to say that Ubud has much to offer. We can wander from one museum to another, admiring the lovely paintings. We can sample a vast range of tasty dishes at the many excellent restaurants. We can observe animal behavior in the Monkey Forest. Or if we want to enjoy stunning views of a tropical paradise, we can stroll along the banks of the Oos River.

Even more interesting, we can simply stay in our hotel room and still absorb the calming atmosphere of Ubud, or sit by the edge of a rice field, enjoying the gentle breezes and the delightful sounds of animals. All this brings us a spiritual experience that's difficult to express in words. We feel at peace, at one with the Creator and the natural environment.

This is the *taksu* of Ubud, which is hard to find anywhere else.

Only in Ubud can we enjoy a vertical experience with God and at the same time the positive horizontal relationships with other humans and with our natural surroundings.

Here we can simultaneously sharpen our Intelligence Quotient (IQ), our Emotional Intelligence Quotient (EQ), and our Spiritual Quotient (SQ).

Our IQ will be enhanced because Ubud is a highly inspiring place to seek out new ideas that we might never have imagined. The diverse population of Ubud, comprising the indigenous Hindu-Bali community, expatriate residents, and tourists, forces us to be more sensitive to and tolerant of others (EQ). And of course, Ubud is an ideal place to develop our inner spirituality (SQ). "Spirituality" here refers not to the formal aspects of religion, but rather to an awareness of ourselves as humans, as creatures. Thus, anyone can experience this spirituality, whatever their religion or beliefs.

If IQ is Mindware, EQ is Heartware, and SQ is Soulware, then taken together they constitute what we call Humanware. Together, these three sets of "equipment" shape us into complete, integrated persons.

The hard work and wisdom of their ancestors, which has been continued and maintained by the community leaders and all the residents of Ubud, has made Ubud a perfect place to develop Humanware. And because Ubud is in Bali, the character of Bali's nature, culture and society strongly influences the creation of this Humanware. It's appropriate, then, that we consider Ubud "**The Spirit of Bali**".

This is why we have written this book and entitled it *Ubud: The Spirit of Bali*. This book examines the various aspects that give Ubud such a unique spirit and character, so difficult to match anywhere else. By learning more about Ubud, perhaps we can gain inspiration that will instill in us the same spirit and character as that found in Ubud.

We've written this book based on knowledge and direct personal experience from being in Ubud, supplemented by supporting information from various written sources.

The book comprises nine chapters, plus the Prologue you are now reading and an Epilogue at the end. We have deliberately divided it into an odd number of chapters, in line with the belief in Hindu-Bali philosophy that odd numbers symbolize balance and harmony.

Here's a brief summary of the chapter contents:

In this Prologue, we explain the background to the book and outline its organization.

In Chapter One, "Welcome to Ubud!", we take you on a short tour around Ubud to become acquainted with some of its tourism attractions and other interesting places. We also examine how Ubud's *taksu* has long enchanted the outside world.

Chapter Two, "The Virtues of Leadership", describes the role of Ubud's leaders, from the birth of Ubud under the guidance of a holy man named Rsi Markandya to the time Ubud started to become better known to the outside world, during the time of the last King of Ubud, Tjokorda Gde Agung Sukawati. This chapter also discusses the role of this last King of Ubud and of his three sons in preserving Balinese culture and improving the prosperity of the local community.

In Chapter Three, "Home of the Legendary Artists", we tell about the role of the pioneering artists—Walter Spies, Rudolf Bonnet, Antonio Blanco, Arie Smit, and I Gusti Nyoman Lempad—and the Pita Maha artists' association that made Ubud famous as the cultural heart of Bali.

In Chapter Four, "Treasures in Museums", we describe various museums in Ubud: Museum Puri Lukisan, Museum Blanco, Museum Rudana, Museum Neka, and Museum ARMA. We also pay a visit to the historic Rumah Lempad. These museums not only house and exhibit collections of priceless art works, but are works of art in themselves, an inseparable part of the development of culture in Ubud.

Chapter Five, "Religious and Spiritual Life", describes the spirit of the people of Ubud in performing their traditional religious ceremonies, how this shapes the character of Ubud, and how it ultimately produces Ubud's deep *taksu*. In this chapter, we explain about Pura Gunung Lebah, the oldest temple in Ubud; the philosophy of the *Banjar* as the core of the traditional community; and the *Pelebon* or *Ngaben* ceremony and the *Odalan* ceremony, just two of the major cultural-religious ceremonies in Ubud.

In Chapter Six, "The Food Paradise", we visit some of Ubud's best known restaurants: Murni's Warung, Warung Babi Guling Ibu Oka, Nasi Ayam Kedewatan Ibu Mangku, Café Wayan, Bebek Bengil, Restoran Indus, Casa Luna, Mozaic, Naughty Nuri's, Jazz Café, Café Lotus, Terazo, and many others. The culinary arts, too, have contributed to shaping Ubud's unique cultural character.

In Chapter Seven, "Natural and Societal Attractions", we describe the philosophy of *Tri Hita Karana* and its direct application to the environment and society in several places and institutions. The places we explore are Pasar Ubud, Jalan Kajeng, Desa Penestanan, the Monkey Forest, Desa Kokokan, Bali Bird Walks, the Tjampuhan Hills, Ubud Botanic Garden, Ubud Organic Market, Pondok Pekak, Pelangi School, and IDEP Foundation.

Chapter Eight, "From Ubud for the World", presents several international-scale events and institutions that have made Ubud even more famous in the global community: the Ubud Writers & Readers Festival, Bali Institute for Renewal (Global Healing Conferences), Bali Spirit Festival, and Humanitad Foundation. Here we also discuss the yoga practices and healing treatment facilities that have become so popular in Ubud in the past few years.

In Chapter Nine, "Business with Values", we describe the business practices prevailing in Ubud, taking as our example the management of the hotels in the Pita Maha hotel group: Hotel Tjampuhan, Hotel Pita Maha, and Hotel Royal Pita Maha. Not coincidentally, this hotel group is owned by the royal family of Ubud. Here we observe the practices of social entrepreneurs, Ubud style.

Finally, in the Epilogue we review the *Tri Hita Karana* philosophy and its application, both to the current context and to the future development of Ubud.

Obviously, we could not have completed this book by ourselves; it has required help, support and cooperation, in many forms and from many people. We'd like to take this opportunity to thank all of them.

First of all, we would like to thank Tjok 'De, who first introduced us to and then made us fall in love with Ubud. From him, we have gained many highly meaningful insights about all aspects of life in Ubud.

Likewise to Tjok Putra, whose full name is Drs. Tjokorda Gde Putra Sukawati, as *Penggelisir,* or respected elder of the entire Royal House of Ubud (Puri Ubud); and to Tjok Ace, whose full name is Dr. Ir. Tjokorda Gde Oka Artha Ardana (AA) Sukawati, MSi, the Regent of Gianyar. These two, who are Tjok 'De's older brothers, deepened our perspective on the cultural, religious, societal and governmental aspects of Ubud.

We'd also like to express our thanks to two other members of the Royal House of Ubud: Tjokorda Raka Kerthyasa, S.Sos., M.Si., better known as Tjok Ibah, and Dr. Ir. Tjokorda Raka Sukawati "Sosrobahu". These two, respected figures in Ubud's community, also work outside Ubud in their respective fields, thereby helping disseminate the spirit of Ubud even more widely.

Next, we'd like to thank various community figures we have met in Ubud, including Nyoman Rudana, Putu Rudana, Suteja Neka, Agung Rai, Mario Blanco, the family of Nyoman Lempad, Ibu Mangku, Ibu Oka, Ketut Liyer, and many others. Their stories have given us great inspiration about Ubud's past and present development.

Our special appreciation goes to Pande Sutawan, Sales and Marketing Director of the Pita Maha Hotel Group. Thanks to Pak Pande, we were able to travel around Ubud and meet many people.

And of course we want to thank all the staff of the Hotel Tjampuhan, Hotel Pita Maha, and Hotel Royal Pita Maha, who served us with such friendliness and sincerity when we stayed at their hotels while writing this book.

We thank our publisher PT Gramedia Pustaka Utama, and especially Dwi Helly Purnomo, for their help in publishing this book, and also our colleagues at MarkPlus, Inc for their suggestions and ideas regarding the business and marketing angles.

It goes without saying that we also offer our deepest thanks to all the residents of Ubud, whom we cannot name one by one. We learned so much from them while preparing this book, and so we dedicate this book to Ubud and all its people.

We also take this opportunity to express our sincerest apologies for any errors or omissions that may have occurred during the writing of this book, which were of course unintentional.

In closing, we hope that this book will serve as a time capsule of Ubud today, which will still be relevant in the years, decades, and even centuries to come.

We hope this book will help everyone gain a deeper understanding of Ubud, and at the same time contribute to Ubud's future development.

May peace be always with us—within us, between humans, and in the entire universe.

Om Shanti Shanti Shanti Om…

Jakarta, December 2009

Hermawan Kartajaya
Bembi Dwi Indrio M.

XVIII
Ubud: The Spirit of Bali

(Endnotes)

1   For a more extensive discussion of Marketing 3.0, see *Marketing 3.0: From Products to Customers to the Human Spirit* by Philip Kotler, Hermawan Kartajaya and Iwan Setiawan. An abbreviated version of this book was published by PT Gramedia Pustaka Utama in 2007, and the full version is to be published on April 2010 by John Wiley & Sons.

Chapter 1

Welcome To Ubud!

"Ubud is the kind of place where a stay of days turns into weeks."
Lonely Planet

Who hasn't heard of Bali?

The island of Bali, with an area of 5,632.86 square kilometers—only 0.3% of Indonesia's land mass—is famous throughout the world. In some countries, the name Bali is more familiar than that of Indonesia; many people don't realize that Bali is a fairly small island in a large country called Indonesia.

This may be because of Bali's long history as a tourism destination, which began long before the Republic of Indonesia was declared. Early in the twentieth century, the Dutch steamship line Koninklijke Paketvaart Maatschappij (KPM) began bringing tourists to visit Bali, through the port of Buleleng in North Bali. These ships had in fact been operating since the nineteenth century, but carrying only cargoes of pigs, copra and coffee, not tourists.

Some time around 1914, KPM published its first brochures promoting tourism in Bali. Then, in 1925, KPM built the first hotel in Bali, the Bali Hotel in Denpasar. Ever since, Bali has been known as an exotic tourist destination.[1]

Foreign tourists started to flock to Bali, enticed by the island's exotic allure, its unique culture, its beautiful scenery, and its friendly people.

They told their friends and relatives, some wrote about Bali in various media, and gradually Bali became famous.

Bali's strategic location has made it a meeting point for many peoples. Bali lies at the crossroads of two oceans—the Indian Ocean and the Pacific—and of two continents—Asia and Australia.

Greater numbers of visitors started coming to Bali after Ngurah Rai Airport was renovated. The airport was first opened in 1931, but was expanded into a modern international airport (by reclaiming land from the sea for runways 1000 meters long) and inaugurated on 1 August 1969. This modern airport opened Bali up to a massive influx of visitors from the outside world.

Yet Bali's special charm remains strong. U.S. President Barack Obama is said to have spent several months in seclusion in Bali while finishing his first book, *Dreams from My Father*. The *New York Times* reports that Obama and his wife Michelle stayed in Bali in the early 1990s completing the book, which was published in 1995. Obama's half-sister Maya Soetoro-Ng, whose father was Indonesian, said that Obama went to Bali after graduating from Harvard Law School "to find a peaceful sanctuary where there were no phones".

Indeed, Bali has long been a favorite destination for those who want to escape the exhausting hustle and bustle of modern life. It's been given many nicknames: the Island of Thousand Temples, the Last Paradise, the Island of Gods, the Morning of the World, the Island of Peace, the Ultimate Island, and the Island of Creativity, to mention but a few.

Introducing Ubud

Bali has several well-known areas, each with a different character. Unlike Kuta, which is "physically wild", or Nusa Dua, which is "professionally peaceful", Ubud is "naturally spiritual".

If we compare Bali to an onion, the skin and outer layers would be Kuta and Nusa Dua, while the innermost layer is Ubud. What is most obvious from the outside, and therefore most often visited by tourists, are places such as Kuta and Nusa Dua, but the true essence of Bali is in Ubud.

Both physically and non-physically, we immediately sense that Ubud is different from the other parts of Bali.

The aura permeating Ubud is truly different from that in other parts of Bali. It feels authentic, warm, friendly, and spiritual. The physical features all contribute to this atmosphere: rice fields, cliffs, rivers, hills, villages, artist communities, temples, palaces, and much more.

But more importantly, the local community strongly maintains its original culture, along with its cultural products in the form of both arts and traditions. It is for this reason that Ubud is recognized as "Bali's Cultural Capital", "Bali's Cultural Heartland".

Geographically, Ubud's location is also quite strategic, as it lies near the center of the island of Bali, making it a convenient base for exploring other areas. It's no wonder that Ubud has become a favorite destination for all types of travelers: backpackers, bohemians, artists and art lovers, anthropologists, writers, yogis, culinary adventurers, celebrities, and ordinary people who just want to enjoy a relaxing holiday.

The local people are engaged in a wide variety of occupations. Some sell things in the market, serve guests in hotels, or guide tourists in museums; others paint, carve wood, tend flocks of ducks, carry baskets on their heads, dance, prepare traditional religious ceremonies, and so on.

It's fair to say that Ubud has become a global village. People from all nationalities and all walks of life can be found here. Ubud is like a canvas full of color.

In governmental terms, the name Ubud refers to two different administrative regions: one is a district (*kecamatan*), while the other is a subdistrict (*kelurahan*), both within the regency (*kabupaten)* of Gianyar.

Ubud District has an area of 42.38 square kilometers, while Ubud Subdistrict is only 7.32 km^2. Apart from Ubud Subdistrict, Ubud District contains seven villages (*desa*): Kedewatan, Petulu, Sayan, Singakerta, Peliatan, Lodtunduh, and Mas.[2] So don't be confused if some people tell you that Mas is in Ubud, while others say it's not; they're both right, but using different references. In this book, we use "Ubud" mostly to refer to Ubud Subdistrict, the heart of Ubud.

Ubud District has a population of around 62,000, of whom around 11,000 live in Ubud Subdistrict. The number of visitors is difficult to estimate, since some people simply pass through, while others stay with relatives or in local people's homes and are therefore not included in official records. [3]

The local community of Ubud is famous for maintaining their cultural traditions. In daily life, most men still wear traditional Balinese clothing: a headcloth or *udeng*, a t-shirt or short-sleeved shirt, and a sarong. For ceremonies, they may dress more formally, with another cloth covering the sarong (*tukad*). Women usually wear traditional blouses (*kebaya*) with a length of cloth wrapped around the body as a skirt (*kain*), and many wear their hair in the traditional bun (*sanggul*).

This reveals the strong character of Ubud's populace. Despite the strong influence of outsiders' clothing styles, the residents of Ubud do not simply copy them; they decide for themselves which influences are appropriate and which are not.

Ubud is full of museums and art galleries of all sizes. Every building, whether a home, an office building, or even a simple food stall, is also full of art works—paintings or wood carvings. And nearly every day, traditional religious ceremonies can be seen. Ubud is often called a "living museum", and it's true: in Ubud, we don't just see museums in the form of buildings containing art works; Ubud itself is indeed a living museum, where the local culture and traditions continue to thrive.

Yet after several visits, we realized that the attractions of Ubud go well beyond its arts, culture and traditions. Ubud is also an ideal place to treat one's physical, emotional, or spiritual ailments. The name Ubud itself comes from the word *ubad*, meaning "medicine". Ubud lies at the confluence of two branches of the Oos River—Oos Kiwa and Oos Tengen—which considered sacred by Balinese. For this reason, Ubud is identified with health and healing.

This is why Ubud is also famous as a spiritual retreat and a place of healing. Many activities relating to these topics have taken place here, such as the Quest for Global Healing conferences. These conferences, initiated by Marcia Jaffe, have been held twice in Ubud, in 2004 and 2006, and were attended by thousands of participants from all religions and all parts of the world.

And indeed, Ubud does have a very peaceful, spiritual atmosphere. Visiting Ubud makes us feel reborn, as if we have rediscovered the meaning of life; we are restored to full functioning, like a car after a thorough overhaul.

If we refer to the concept of holistic well-being, with a proper balance of physical, emotional and spiritual health, it's fair to say that Ubud offers a complete "health care package". To maintain our physical fitness, we can hike along the banks of the Oos River (also often called the Tjampuhan River because it is in the Tjampuhan area) while enjoying the beautiful views of nature. Or if we're not feeling that fit, we can enjoy a spa and massage treatment at one of the many venues in Ubud.

To enhance our sensitivity toward others (the emotional aspect), we can interact with the heterogeneous, open community of Ubud. And for our spiritual health, we can visit museums, watch arts performances, or practice yoga and meditation.

Ubud's atmosphere allows us to escape the pressures of urban life. The air in Ubud is fresh, as it's situated in the hills, and the skies are clear, because there's very little air pollution. Our imagination can carry us anywhere as we gaze into the blue sky with pure white clouds majestically drifting by.

The community of Ubud, as part of the greater community of Bali, has long been aware of the importance of seeking this inspiration in daily life. There are gazebos called *bale bengong*, where people can simply relax and contemplate life. *Bale* means "abode", while *bengong* means "emptying one's mind", "becoming lost in thought".

Around Ubud

So what is there to see and do in Ubud?

We're going to take you on a short tour of Ubud. Ubud isn't a very big area, so we can quickly get acquainted with the major points of interest. And the population is fairly small, so we can easily get to know the local people as well.

We start our tour right between Puri Ubud (the palace) and Pasar Ubud (the market), at the intersection of the main roads: Jalan Raya Ubud, Jalan Suweta, and Jalan Monkey Forest. We choose this as our reference point because it is usually the drop-off point for vehicles that bring tourists to Ubud; we can consider it "kilometer zero" for Ubud.

Figure 1.1 Ubud Corner

The most interesting place here is of course the palace, Puri Saren Agung Ubud, usually just called Puri Ubud. This is the residence of the kings of Ubud and their families. The last King of Ubud was Tjokorda Gde Agung Sukawati (1910-1978). The palace courtyard is also the venue for nightly arts performances.

Figure 1.2 Puri Ubud

Aside from the Ubud Subdistrict government office, this is also the location of the Tourism Information Centre, where we can find all kinds of information about Ubud. Across from it is the *wantilan*, a sort of open-air village hall, where drivers and tour guides can often be seen resting. In this area there are many "taxis" with drivers ready to take you wherever you want to go, and in the afternoon and evening the area swarms with local people offering tickets to the cultural performances.

Figure 1.3 Ubud Tourism Information Centre

Still in this immediate area, next to the *wantilan*, is Ibu Oka's famous Warung Babi Guling, a food stall selling roast suckling pig. To the north, along Jalan Suweta, are the Bumbu Bali and Terazo restaurants, and the gallery of Rio Helmi, a renowned photographer who records the culture, nature and people of Bali. A bit further on is one of Ubud's main temples, Pura Puseh Ubud.

Heading to the west, along Jalan Raya Ubud, we come to the painting museum, Museum Puri Lukisan. Along this five-meter-wide cobbled road are two more *pura*—Pura Desa Ubud and Pura Dalem Ubud, a row of restaurants including Ary's Warung, Casa Luna, and Café Lotus, and the Kunang-Kunang antique shop.

Figure 1.4 Jalan Raya Ubud

If you continue westward, you pass through a sort of natural tunnel formed by dense, curving bamboo trees and the dangling roots of other plants. On the other side of the tunnel is the bridge crossing over the Oos River; here Jalan Raya Ubud changes its name and becomes Jalan Raya Sanggingan.

Figure 1.5 Ubud "Tunnel"
Figure 1.6 Ubud Bridge

On Jalan Raya Sanggingan, often also called Jalan Raya Tjampuhan, are more restaurants—Murni's Warung and The Bridge—and the Museum Blanco. Right next to the museum is the road leading to Penestanan village, famous for its community of painters who work in the "Young Artist" style.

Continuing north, we come to several hotels: Hotel Ibah, Hotel Tjampuhan, and Hotel Pita Maha. The historic Hotel Tjampuhan is situated next to Pura Gunung Lebah, one of Bali's oldest temples, and was formerly the home of the famous painter Walter Spies.

Still on Jalan Raya Sanggingan are several more well-known restaurants, including Indus, Mozaic, and Naughty Nuri's, and the Museum Neka. There's also a spot beside the road called the "Art Zoo", selling paintings of such famous personages as Barack Obama, Mahatma Gandhi, Mona Lisa, Che Guevara, Albert Einstein, and Bob Marley.

Jalan Raya Sanggingan then turns left and becomes Jalan Lungsiakan. At the western end of Jalan Lungsiakan is a three-way intersection. If you turn right, you're on Jalan Raya Kedewatan; to the left, it's Jalan Raya Sayan.

On Jalan Raya Kedewatan are several luxurious hotels, such as the Hotel Royal Pita Maha, Kupu-Kupu Barong, Alila Ubud, Komaneka Resort, COMO Shambala, and Ubud Hanging Gardens; along Jalan Raya Sayan is another row of luxury hotels: Amandari, Four Seasons, The Mansion, and Kayumanis. Also on Jalan Raya Sayan is a place called Sayan Terrace that is famous for its beautiful views and therefore a popular spot for photography.

These hotels have well-established international reputations. The Hotel Royal Pita Maha has extensive convention center facilities, while the swimming pool at the Hotel Alila Ubud was chosen by *Travel + Leisure* magazine as one of the "50 Most Spectacular Pools in the World".

Also at Jalan Raya Kedewatan, we can go river rafting down the Ayung River, or have some famous chicken and rice at Warung Nasi Ayam Kedewatan Ibu Mangku or Warung Nasi Ayam Kedewatan Ibu Mardika.

Figure 1.7 Ayung River Valley

Now let's start again from the corner near Puri Ubud and Pasar Ubud.

This time, we head east. First we come to the ever-busy traditional market, Pasar Ubud. Across the road is the home of the late I Gusti Nyoman Lempad, one of Bali's great art maestros, and next to it the

Rendezvous Doux restaurant, which often shows old documentary films about Bali such as Miguel Covarrubias's silent film "Bali 1930s".

Heading eastward along Jalan Raya Ubud we come to Nomad restaurant, Neka Gallery, and several banks. The road ends at a three-way intersection with a giant statue of Arjuna.

Figure 1.8 Giant Statue of Arjuna

From this intersection, on the road heading north, Jalan Andong, are more luxury hotels, such as Kamandalu and The Viceroy. Also in this area are tourist spots such as the Ubud Botanical Garden and Desa Kokokan (White Heron Village). On the road heading south, Jalan Raya Peliatan, are even more luxury hotels, Maya Ubud and The Chedi Club, and one of Ubud's best-known museums, Museum Rudana.

Returning to Pasar Ubud, this time we go south, along Jalan Hanoman. As well as art and souvenir shops, this road is lined with restaurants, including Restoran Bebek Bengil (Dirty Duck Diner). If we turn westward at this restaurant, we head toward Jalan Wanara Wana, better known as Monkey Forest Road, which leads to the monkey forest, officially called Mandala Wisata Wanara Wana (Sacred Monkey Forest Sanctuary).

If we continue along this road, it curves northward and takes us back toward the intersection with Puri Ubud and Pasar Ubud, past more art galleries and souvenir shops, as well as shops selling gold and silver jewelry such as Seraphim and Ada-Ada Silver. Along the Monkey Forest Road are many restaurants, including Café Wayan and a Danish restaurant that sells homemade ice cream.

Figure 1.9 Jalan Monkey Forest

Also on Monkey Forest Road is the Ubud Football Field, where local people play soccer or fly kites in the afternoons. The field is also used for special events that involve large numbers of people. Next to the field is a small library called Pondok Pekak.

Now let's go back to the area near Restoran Bebek Bengil. If, instead of turning onto the Monkey Forest Road, you continue south on Jalan Raya Pengosekan, you come to Museum ARMA and several restaurants, including Pizza Bagus, Warung Enak, and Warung Opera. This is also the stop for the Perama shuttle bus, popular with backpackers. Continuing south, you come to the Artists Community led by I Dewa Nyoman Batuan.

That concludes our lightning tour of the main sights of Ubud.

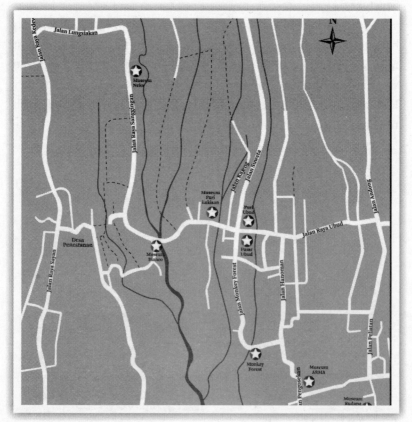

Figure 1.10 Map of Ubud

Facilities in Ubud

Apart from the places described above, many spas, yoga facilities and healing centers have recently appeared in many parts of Ubud, from the most basic to those in the luxury hotels.

While Kuta is generally crowded with tourists, in Ubud we can stroll quite comfortably along the roads, and there aren't too many motor vehicles.

And while we're discussing facilities, most tourist places in Ubud— shops, hotels and restaurants—now accept payment by credit or debit card. And if you run out of cash, there are plenty of ATMs.

There are a couple of fairly large supermarkets, Bintang and Delta Dewata, convenience stores such as Circle K, and of course the many small shops in and around Pasar Ubud, so there's no problem meeting your normal daily needs.

You can also access the internet at small shops called *warnet* ("warung internet"), and many hotels and restaurants have wi-fi facilities. If you need reading material, there are plenty of new and used bookstores: Periplus, Ganesha Bookshop, Adi Bookshop, and Ary's Bookshop.

What about food?

Not to worry. As we mentioned earlier, Ubud is teeming with warungs, restaurants, and cafés of all types. Whatever you want, you can probably find it: traditional Balinese dishes, specialties from other regions of Indonesia, and Asian and Western cuisine from many different countries.

And though we've mentioned many luxury hotels, if you happen to be on a more limited budget, or even one of those backpackers, there's plenty of accommodation for you as well. While Ubud is often perceived as an expensive tourist area, there are many lodgings at more affordable rates, particularly along Jalan Kajeng, Jalan Gautama, Jalan Jembawan, Jalan Bisma, and in Desa Penestanan.

Figure 1.11 Jalan Bisma

The weather in Ubud is fairly normal for Indonesia: it's hot in the daytime, and cooler but not too cold at night. But the air is fresher and less polluted, because there are so many trees and relatively few vehicles.

And this makes Ubud quite a pleasant place for walking, bicycling or, for longer trips, motorcycling. The various tourist destinations are not too far apart, and by walking we can better soak up and savor Ubud's atmosphere.

If you want to go somewhere a bit further away, you can take an unofficial taxi. Drivers are constantly coming up to you and saying "*Do you need transport, Sir?*" or "*Taxi, Sir?*", while making a gesture with both hands as if steering a car.

From the marketing perspective, Ubud has excellent access, in the sense that it's very easy to get there and very convenient to walk around once you're there. Ubud also offers personalized service, in that you can decide for yourself what you want to do while you're there.

So that's a very brief overview of some of the interesting places in the Ubud area. Of course, due to the limited space here, it's far from complete; in any corner of Ubud, on some narrow lane, you're always finding something new—a house with interesting architecture, a food stall serving unique dishes, or an art shop with top-quality products.

Information about Ubud is readily available, since there are information centers and travel agents everywhere. And the local people of Ubud, called Ubudians, are very friendly and helpful; tourists can ask almost anyone for help, because English is widely spoken, at least to a certain level.

One of the best things about Ubud is that, unlike in most other places, we can be "active" rather than just "passive" tourists. As well as simply visiting museums, watching cultural performances, and sampling food in restaurants, we can also participate directly in these activities, by learning to paint at certain museums and galleries, studying dance or music at local studios, or taking cooking lessons at restaurants and cafés.

We can also take part in simpler but equally enjoyable activities such as planting rice or climbing coconut trees to pick the fruit. These activities are part of daily life for rural people, but unusual and therefore memorable for urban dwellers. And these basic activities not only bring us simple pleasures, but make us reflect on the meaning behind them.

On the other hand, to protect Ubud's *taksu,* certain activities commonly found in other tourist areas are not allowed in Ubud. There are no night clubs or movie theaters. The restaurants and cafés all close by around eleven in the evening, rather than staying open till the break of dawn. This is to prevent people from becoming too deeply involved in worldly pursuits, and also so that the local wildlife is not disturbed by the loud music that night clubs usually produce.

You also won't find any fast food restaurants or global food and beverage outlets in Ubud—places like KFC, McDonald's, or Starbucks—since these are considered inconsistent with the values of Ubud's community. Not only would they reduce patronage at the food outlets run by the local people, but they would also generate a lot of material—plastic bags, cups and so on—that would gradually degrade the environment of Ubud. For these reasons, the local government issues no permits for such places.

Modern shopping malls are also not allowed, as they would disrupt the economic system, and the interpersonal relationships, of the local community. The goods sold in modern shopping centers typically come from large-scale producers, rather than from the local community, and therefore would produce no benefit for the people of Ubud. Modern shopping centers also lack the bargaining between sellers and buyers that is a normal form of social interaction in this traditional society.

These restrictions are a manifestation of the *Tri Hita Karana* philosophy embraced by the people of Ubud. But these restrictions do not deter visitors to Ubud; quite the contrary. Many people come to Ubud because they are bored with fast food outlets and shopping malls, and they like Ubud precisely because it is so unspoiled and authentic.

Ubud: The Best Part of Bali

Ubud is, then, a kind of antithesis of the usual modern urban lifestyle. Here we can indulge in contemplation and refocus on our inner selves, rather than enduring the constant barrage of modern external stimuli. The ambience supports this; it's tranquil and far removed from the bustle of urban life. Time seems to move more slowly; there's no hurry, stress, anxiety, or pressing deadlines.

With its innate *taksu*, Ubud enchanted many world-class artists in the past, including Walter Spies, Rudolf Bonnet, Antonio Blanco, Arie Smit, Han Snel, Colin McPhee, and many others. Now, too, Ubud has attracted not only artists but people from many other professions, such as Janet DeNeefe (owner of Indus and Casa Luna restaurants and initiator of the Ubud Writers & Readers Festival), Chris Salans (cook and owner of Mozaic restaurant), Victor Mason (ornithologist), Rucina Ballinger (dance ethnographer and writer), Meghan Pappenheim (co-founder of Bali Spirit Festival), and Rio Helmi (photographer). And such people are magnets who in turn attract others, especially expatriates, to come to Ubud.

It's not surprising that so much has been written about Ubud. Standard information about Ubud is provided in all the leading travel guides, such as *Lonely Planet, The Rough Guide,* and *Frommer's.* More detailed descriptions of the culture, history and society of Ubud are available in the books *Ubud Is A Mood* from the Bali Purnati Center for the Arts, *Ubud and Beyond* by Richard Mann, and *Kembang Rampai Desa Ubud (Anthology on the Village of Ubud)* by Ir. Tjokorda Oka A.A. Sukawati, M.Si. et al. Information on Ubud can also be found on many Internet websites.

Ubud has also been the setting for several literary works. For example, Ubud is featured as the scene of a current New York Times best seller entitled *Eat Pray Love: One Woman's Search for Everything* by Elizabeth Gilbert, and there are plans to make the book into a film starring Julia Roberts and Javier Bardem.

Over the past decade, Ubud has been the venue for many annual international events relating to cultural, spiritual, and environmental matters, including the Ubud Writers & Readers Festival, the Bali Spirit Festival, and the Global Healing Conference (now named the Bali Institute for Global Renewal).

In 2010, Ubud will be host to an international business meeting, the Pan-Pacific Conference XXVII held by the Pan-Pacific Business Association based at the University of Nebraska at Lincoln. The purpose of the conference is to discuss important matters relating to the quality of life in the Pan-Pacific region—a theme entirely in line with the values expressed in the daily lives of the people of Ubud.

Ubud is indeed a very special place—not just for us, but for people from all around the world. The *National Geographic Traveler* has written that "Ubud is the best part of Bali".[4]

This survey was based on studies by 522 experts on sustainable tourism and destinations on the conditions in 111 islands and island groups around the world. It assessed the qualities that make a destination unique—not just basic matters such as the service in the hotels.

Overall, Bali achieved a score of 57 out of a possible 100, indicating that Bali as a whole has both positive and negative sides in terms of sustainable tourism. As one of the experts polled in the survey wrote, "Bali is a mixed bag of tourism projects that represent the absolute worst (Kuta) in sustainable travel and some of the best (Ubud)."

And in fact, despite a near-total lack of large-scale promotion (for example through advertising), Ubud is a well-recognized "brand", with strong credibility. This is an example of what, in the concept of New Wave Marketing, we call "low-budget, high-impact marketing".[5] Ubud's strong character makes it a topic of endless discussion.

Obviously, this has not happened overnight; it has developed continually since the village of Ubud was first founded. But the values that have always imbued Ubud's society have survived and persisted, because the entire community, at all levels, upholds them so wholeheartedly.

And this is why Ubud has been able to grow without losing its innate character. Some outside influences are accepted, as long as they are in line with the basic values embraced by the community of Ubud. This has created a genuine process of growth and development, with harmonious synergy between the past and the present, between tradition and modern life, and between Eastern and Western cultures.

Ubud is indeed The Spirit of Bali...

(Endnotes)

1   Data from the Gianyar Regency website, http://www.gianyarkab.go.id.

2   Ibid.

3   As well as the numbers of passengers passing through airports and seaports, official tourist visit figures are usually based on the numbers of hotel guests.

4   Information from *National Geographic Traveler* magazine, November–December 2007.

5   For more on the concept of New Wave Marketing, see the book *New Wave Marketing* by Hermawan Kartajaya, published by PT Gramedia Pustaka Utama in December 2008.

Chapter 2

The Virtues of Leadership

*"Agung (Tjokorda Gde Agung Sukawati, the King of Ubud)—
tall and high a volcanic soul—thus you create yourself into
a towering pose clad in a magic mist..."*
Comment by J. Siegrist, a visitor to Puri Ubud in the 1960s

"The fishermen see Amad Mohamad passing above them on his flying horse."

That's basically what we see in a painting now in the Museum Puri Lukisan in Ubud—a work by Ida Bagus Bala (1887–1942) from Batuan, Sukawati, entitled "Fishermen See Amad on His Flying Horse," painted in 1931.

This painting, done in ink on paper, portrays the daily lives of the people of Bali as they observe someone passing overhead on a flying horse. This person, Amad, is riding a flying horse and carrying a golden whip, which he obtained from a magical tree on a mysterious island. Witnessed by a fisherman out at sea, Amad flies into the heavens, pursuing a princess who stole his other magical possessions while he was sleeping.

What is so interesting about this painting, which was donated to the museum by one of Ubud's master artists, Rudolf Bonnet?

To us, this painting suggests the influence of Islamic and Arabic culture in Hindu-Bali society at that time. It's fairly easy to guess that the name "Amad Mohamad" in the painting derives from that of the prophet Muhammad.

And Ida Bagus Bala was not the only local artist to portray this character Amad Mohamad in his paintings. There is another painting entitled "Amad's Three Magical Possessions," by Ida Bagus Togog (1913–1989), who was also from Batuan, Sukawati. This painting, done in tempera on plywood in 1937, show us Amad's three magical possessions that were stolen by Princess Beregedab while he was sleeping.

The three magical possessions are an arrow that returns to its owner after hitting its target; a bag that is always full of food; and a garment that enables the person who wears it to fly.

We feel these paintings are extremely significant. They show how open Balinese artists of that time were to accepting influences from outside Hindu-Balinese culture and incorporating them into their works. This indicates a receptiveness toward a variety of cultures, as long as these are perceived to be in line with Hindu-Balinese values.

It is this outward-looking perspective, while still upholding the original local culture and values, that has enabled Ubud to preserve its special identity. The people of Ubud do not automatically absorb just anything that outsiders bring in, but neither do they instinctively reject all outside influences.

Rsi Markandya: The Demigod Founder

If we look further back, the inhabitants of Bali, and of Ubud, were actually once newcomers themselves. The Hindu-Balinese we know today are in fact descendants of Javanese who emigrated to Bali many centuries ago.

According to historical sources, as early as 1343 Bali was part of the Majapahit kingdom, which was centered in East Java. Hindu influence began to spread among the original inhabitants of Bali, who were followers of what was called "the Old Religion".

When Majapahit collapsed in 1515, the small Islamic kingdoms on Java united and formed a new kingdom, the Islamic kingdom of Mataram. Recognizing their loss of political power, the remnants of the

Majapahit royal family and their retinues migrated across the straits to Bali. They were Majapahit's elite: the royal family, nobles, priests, artists, and soldiers. And because they are descended from this elite, the Balinese of today remain proud of their heritage.[1]

But Ubud itself was founded long before this influx from Majapahit. The story of the origin of the village of Ubud is related in a set of *lontar* (a sacred manuscript written on palm leaves) called the *Markandya Purana*. According to this chronicle, the pioneer who founded Ubud and its civilization was a holy man named Mahayogi Markandya, or Rsi Markandya.[2]

Rsi Markandya was a Hindu priest who had come from India. He arrived in the Indonesian archipelago in around the 11th century CE[3] and lived in the mountains at Gunung Rawung (now called Gunung Lawu) in East Java.

Rsi Markandya had many disciples in East Java. One day, as he was meditating at Gunung Rawung, Rsi Markandya received a revelation—a mysterious voice accompanied by a bright light from the East.

He gazed eastward and saw in a vision a row of fertile, green mountains stretching from West to East. The voice whispered that he should come with his followers to the island that was then called Dawa (the name *dawa* comes from Old Javanese and means "long") to open up new land in this long chain of mountains.

And so Rsi Markandya immediately announced this message to his followers. He and around 800 followers decided to migrate to the island of Dawa. Once all their supplies were ready, Rsi Markandya and his companions set out for Dawa.

But they failed to perform the necessary rituals. The Rsi neglected to request permission from the spirits and creatures living on Dawa. And so, when they arrived on Dawa, they were beset by all kinds of misfortunes. Wild animals—tigers, snakes, and so on—attacked many of Rsi Markandya's followers as they passed through the forest. Then an epidemic struck; many more fell ill and died.

Sad and disappointed, Rsi Markandya decided to return to Java with his few remaining followers.

Rsi Markandya again meditated at Gunung Rawung to seek guidance from Ida Sang Hyang Widhi Wasa, the Supreme Creator of the Universe. Eventually he was granted the knowledge that whenever we want to obtain anything, a ritual is required of us. At the end of this meditation, he informed his followers that he planned to return to Dawa.

This time, he took along a number of other Rsi. In this second expedition, around 400 people accompanied him, most of whom were from the village of Aga. They brought farming tools and various plant seedlings, referred to as *sarwapala* ("all foods"), to clear and cultivate the new land.

When they arrived on Dawa, before entering the forest, Rsi Markandya and the other Rsi held a ceremony. They asked Almighty God and their new surroundings to allow them to use this land for agriculture. They also prayed to be protected from disease and wild animals during their journey.

Figure 2.1 A relief on Rsi Markandya's journey

Once Rsi Markandya and the people from Aga village had finished these prayers, they continued by ritually planting the *Pancadatu* (five types of metals—silver, copper, gold, iron, and tin—plus rubies) as a symbol of the five elements, to ensure that the clearing of the new land for farming would be successful. Rsi Markandya gave the name Basuki, meaning "safe, secure," to the place where the Pancadatu were buried. Basuki is now the village of Besakih, on the slopes of the great mountain, Gunung Agung, and the site of Bali's largest temple complex, Pura Besakih.

And as they continued their journey through the island of Dawa, Rsi Markandya gave names to all the places they passed through.

From Gunung Agung, Rsi Markandya headed toward the hills in the West, and found a river with sparkling, clear water. Because there was no road, Rsi Markandya and his disciples followed the course of this river, stopping to meditate at many places along the way. They also regularly bathed in the river, and they discovered that as well as cleansing their bodies, the water of this river gave them great health. According to Rsi Markandya, this river had healing powers.

And so he gave it the name Oos (also sometimes pronounced Wos), an abbreviation of the word *osada* (or *wosada*). The Sanskrit word *osada*, meaning "health", was later adapted to become *ubad*, meaning "medicine". This was the origin of the area now known as Ubud. Because of the important role of holy river water, the Hindu-Bali religion is also sometimes called Agama Tirta, the religion of holy water.

As they traced the river upstream, they found it branched into two. The branch on the left was called Oos Kiwa (meaning "left") and the right branch was called Oos Tengen ("right"). The point where the two branches come together was called Tjampuhan, meaning "mixture" or "confluence".

Figure 2.2 Oos River

At this location, Rsi Markandya and his followers built a temple: Pura Gunung Lebah ("temple in a mountain valley").

From here, he continued north. Arriving in a village, he saw many *bidadari* (nymphs) as lovely as goddesses. The place itself was also very beautiful and imbued with a spiritual atmosphere like that of heaven, the abode of the gods. And so Rsi Markandya named this place Kedewatan (ke-dewa-an, "place of the gods").

Still in this same general area was another swift-flowing river, where Rsi Markandya saw many bidadari bathing, and so he named the river Ayu, meaning "beautiful"; it is now called Sungai Ayung.

Rsi Markandya continued his journey. He came to a place where he distributed land to his followers, and so this village was called Puwakan (meaning "sharing, allocation").

He then continued his journey and came to a dense forest, where he and his disciples rested and performed yoga—this traditional village (*Desa Adat*) is now called Desa Adat Payogan. They pressed on; the next village he named is now Desa Adat Taro, because he taught holy thoughts and teachings there. (The word *taro* or *taru* means "wood". The word *kayu*, meaning "wood", in turn derives from *kayun*, meaning "desire", in this case meaning "having pure and holy desires and ideas".)

Here in Desa Taro, he divided the land reclaimed from the forest into three parts: the *Desa* organization to maintain harmony between humans and God (*Parahyangan*), the *Banjar* organization to maintain good relations among humans (*Pawongan*), and the *Subak* organization to manage agricultural matters, including irrigation systems—in other words, to maintain harmony between humans and the environment (*Palemahan*). This division was aimed at maintaining harmony in this place, and was the origin of the traditional organizations that have been passed down to contemporary society.

The people from Desa Aga who took part in this expedition were called Bali Aga, meaning people from the village of Desa Aga who undertook Wali, or a holy sacrifice. Since then, the island formerly known as Dawa has been called Wali or Bali. Later, the "original" inhabitants of Bali also came to be called Bali Aga.

That, in brief, is the tale of Rsi Markandya, who brought his followers from East Java to the island of Dawa to open up new land, and of how the island came to be known as Bali.

Many traces of the early culture brought by Rsi Markandya can still be seen. Apart from the village names just mentioned, we also see that in their daily lives, the people of Ubud continue to perform traditional religious ceremonies, at all levels from routine to massive; this tendency has persisted since the time of Ubud's founding by Rsi Markandya. We can also see the origins of the Tri Hita Karana philosophy of respect for God, for nature, and for the community of humans.

The story of Rsi Markandya also makes it clear that Ubud has intense *taksu*. Rsi Markandya wandered around Bali and discovered Ubud with no previous references, even though Bali was all virgin forest at the time. He was drawn to Ubud and settled there precisely because he perceived its strongly spiritual aura. This same aura can still be felt in Ubud, despite the changing times.

The King of Ubud

If Rsi Markandya played an important role in initiating the birth of Ubud, its kings and royal family—the house of Puri Ubud—have played a major role in defending and developing spiritual and cultural values in the community.

At many times and in many places throughout the world, kings and their families have enjoyed great respect. Royal families and other nobles have been seen as having a special, and hereditary, relationship with the Almighty. For this reason, they have often had tremendous influence in all aspects of their societies.

This has also been true in Balinese society. The royal families, in Bali called the *puri* families, are deeply respected and honored by their communities. Though they no longer hold official positions in the government, the royal families still have great influence in community life. They are considered the heirs and defenders of local culture and traditions. The culture itself is believed to have been sent down through revelations from the Creator, and art is an important manifestation of this culture. Consequently, the development of art and culture in Bali has been inseparably entwined with the role of the royal families.

This has certainly been the case in Ubud. The family of Puri Ubud has always had a tremendous influence on artistic and cultural developments.

In the early 20th century, Puri Ubud actively opened itself up to outside influences—especially artists from the West—that were felt to be in line with the values of Ubud's society and beneficial for improving the community's living standards. It was then that the outside world started to know about Ubud, and Ubud began to undergo many significant changes.

If the era of Rsi Markandya can be called Ubud 1.0, we can refer to Puri Ubud's era of emergence and receptiveness to the outside world as Ubud 2.0.

By the 1920s, Bali was already quite well known to tourists from Europe and North America, thanks to the heavy promotion by the Dutch, who controlled Indonesia at the time. Bali was publicized for its natural beauty, exotic arts and culture, and ingenuous native people, whose women still went around bare-breasted. The slogan at the time was "Bali is the Last Paradise". The Dutch wanted to make Bali the center of tourism in their colony.

Western tourists began to flock to Ubud. Their presence introduced the people of Ubud to the concept of the tourism industry and gradually helped stimulate the local economy.

The 1920s and 1930s were difficult times for Ubud economically. In 1934, when 24-year-old Tjokorda Gde Agung Sukawati acceded to the throne of Ubud, there was basically nothing in Ubud—no roads at all, let alone motor vehicles.

Figure 2.3 Tjokorda Gde Agung Sukawati (courtesy of Puri Ubud)

As the King of Ubud, Tjokorda Gde Agung Sukawati wanted to improve conditions in his community. He had a vision of attracting foreign tourists to visit and stay in the palace, Puri Ubud. Luckily, he was fluent in English and Dutch, so he formed strong friendships with his foreign visitors.

Tjokorda Gde Agung Sukawati also had a vision of developing the arts in Ubud. In those days, Balinese artists knew virtually nothing about Western art, and conversely, Western artists knew very little about Balinese art. Tjokorda Gde Agung Sukawati thought that if Western artists came to Bali, and specifically to Ubud, Balinese artists could learn from them and Bali's art would become better known to the outside world.

Tjokorda Gde Raka Sukawati, his elder brother, happened to meet Walter Spies at the Kraton of Yogyakarta. Spies was a multi-talented artist who was then studying Javanese music. Tjokorda Gde Raka Sukawati invited Spies to come and stay in Ubud. Walter Spies, and later Rudolf Bonnet, played an important role in developing the arts in Ubud, and in Bali as a whole.

At first, Spies and the other Western artists stayed at Puri Ubud. Later, they lived on various plots of land given to them by Tjokorda Gde Agung Sukawati.

With the arrival of these Western artists, the arts of Bali gradually gained greater recognition. To encourage development of the arts in Ubud, Tjokorda Gde Agung Sukawati regularly held "Bali Nights" for Western tourists at Puri Ubud.

In 1936, to advance the art of painting in Ubud, Tjokorda Gde Agung Sukawati and Tjokorda Gde Raka Sukawati, together with Walter Spies, Rudolf Bonnet, and legendary Balinese painter I Gusti Nyoman Lempad, founded an artists' association called Pita Maha. Later, in the 1950s, Museum Puri Lukisan was built as a place for people to appreciate the paintings produced by the Pita Maha artists.

Figure 2.4 Tjokorda Gde Agung Sukawati with tourists (courtesy of Puri Ubud)

Figure 2.5 Puri Ubud in the 1960s (courtesy of Puri Ubud)

Thanks to these efforts, the outside world began to recognize Ubud as an artistic and cultural center. Its culture and art works attracted great interest. Slowly, Ubud became a tourism destination. Equally important, the arrival of tourists started to build a spirit of entrepreneurship amongst the Ubudians, most of whom were still farmers.

In traditional Balinese society, works of art—paintings and carvings—are part of daily life; art is not considered a dedicated profession or a livelihood aimed at earning money. People create art works for spiritual or religious purposes, to decorate temples or palaces or to be used in religious ceremonies.

The growth of the arts in Ubud experienced a second revival in the 1960s to 1970s, when a leading artist from the Netherlands, Arie Smit, taught painters from Penestanan village in the "Young Artist" style. And in early 1962, Puri Ubud received a visit from the charismatic young Attorney General of the United States, Robert F. Kennedy.

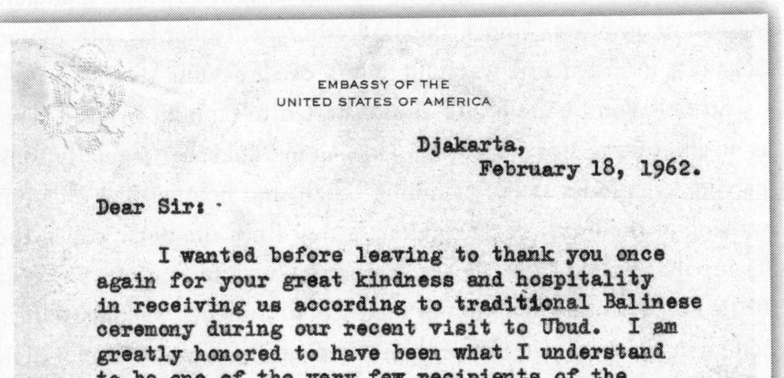

EMBASSY OF THE
UNITED STATES OF AMERICA

Djakarta,
February 18, 1962.

Dear Sir:

I wanted before leaving to thank you once again for your great kindness and hospitality in receiving us according to traditional Balinese ceremony during our recent visit to Ubud. I am greatly honored to have been what I understand to be one of the very few recipients of the Gold Flower.

My wife and I will both treasure the picture you presented to us and I am sure that the President of the United States will also be very grateful for the painting you have presented to him.

Very truly yours,

Robert F. Kennedy
Attorney General of the
United States of America

P.J.M. Tjokorde Agung,
Ubud, Gianjar,
Bali.

Figure 2.6 A letter from Robert F. Kennedy (courtesy of Puri Ubud)

The momentum continued. In the early 1970s, the Indonesian government, under the recently established "New Order" regime, renewed the intensive promotion of tourism to Bali. Ubud experienced a sharp rise in foreign tourist arrivals following visits by Queen Elizabeth II and Prince Philip of the UK, Queen Juliana of the Netherlands, and U.S. Vice President Nelson Rockefeller.

These visits by state dignitaries were covered by the mass media, making the name Ubud more popular abroad. This sparked Ubud's second revival, following that of the '20s and '30s.

As Ubud became better known as an artistic and cultural center and grew as a tourist destination, the living standards of its people gradually started to improve. Under the leadership of Tjokorda Gde Agung Sukawati, infrastructure was built to improve the public's welfare.

Schools and public health clinics started to be built in 1955. This is an interesting story. Tjokorda Gde Agung Sukawati regularly took part in ceremonies at Pura Gunung Lebah, and he often saw children walking at the break of dawn along a trail from the north called the Tjampuhan Ridge Path. He asked what these children were doing. It turned out that they were junior high school students, walking to their school in Gianyar, quite far away. At that time, there was no junior high school in Ubud, let alone a high school; only a state primary school.

So Tjokorda Gde Agung Sukawati donated two plots of land to build junior high schools. One, directly opposite Pura Gunung Lebah, is now called Kerta Yoga Ubud Junior High School (SMP Kerta Yoga Ubud), and the other, opposite Museum Puri Lukisan, is now Ubud State Junior High School 1 (SMP Negeri 1 Ubud). In 1981, a high school (Ubud State High School 1 or SMA Negeri 1 Ubud) was also built on Jalan Suweta by the royal family.

Ubud was thus the pioneer in establishing secondary schools at the district level in Bali. Up to that time, the only secondary schools were in regency-level towns, not in district-level towns such as Ubud.

The schools established by Tjokorda Gde Agung Sukawati now have excellent reputations; Ubud State Junior High School 1 and Ubud State High School 1 are categorized as International-Standard Schools. Both are among the best schools in Bali; places in these schools are eagerly sought by students not only from Ubud but from outlying regions as well.

The establishment of health clinics followed the same pattern. Tjokorda Gde Agung Sukawati was alarmed to see that local residents who were ill had to be transported long distances for treatment, so he donated land to build a medical clinic, now called Klinik Dharma Usada, on Jalan Raya Ubud just above the Ubud "tunnel".[4]

We can see how the vision, entrepreneurial spirit, and social concerns of Tjokorda Gde Agung Sukawati as the King of Ubud helped transform Ubud into a better place for its people. This highly respected King of Ubud passed away in 1978, and was honored with a huge royal cremation ceremony (*Pelebon*).

Figure 2.7 Kerta Yoga Ubud Junior High School

Figure 2.8 Ubud State Junior High School 1

Figure 2.9 Klinik Dharma Usada

The Royal Family in Recent Times

The people of Ubud are very grateful to this last King of Ubud and to the entire royal family for their willingness to open up to the outside world and accept certain outside influences, rather than closing their community off to progress and development. Many in the local community feel that Puri Ubud is different from the other royal houses in Bali. Puri Ubud is genuinely concerned with the people's economic and social welfare.

The family of Puri Ubud remains highly respected in the community, because they do not simply rely on the charisma derived from their noble descent. They also have deep knowledge and skills in the cultural and artistic realms, and involve themselves directly in community social activities such as traditional religious ceremonies. They have had a tremendous impact in maintaining the original architecture of temples and preserving the temples' many important heirlooms, such as the sacred barong. The royal family has succeeded in involving all elements of the *catur wangsa* (the four castes in Hindu-Bali society: Brahmana, Ksatriya, Weisya, and Sudra) in local activities.

Mario Blanco, son of the legendary artist Antonio Blanco, says that the Puri Ubud family always makes substantial contributions, in many ways, to every traditional religious ceremony.

We can see how strongly the king and the royal family of Puri Ubud have influenced Ubud's development. If, back in those early days, the King of Ubud had not opened the area up by inviting foreign artists and giving them places to live, the people of Ubud would never have been willing to let foreign tourists stay in their homes; there were no inns or hotels in Ubud back then.

And interestingly, though the foreign artists and the local artists spoke different languages, this was not a major obstacle. The artists were able to work together effectively because they shared a common language—the language of art.

Even now, the family of Puri Ubud remains a driving force in Ubud's development. They continue to donate art works such as paintings and barong to the various museums, and they are actively involved in all social and community affairs.

The present Puri Ubud family has everything covered: they are involved in social and community affairs, government, business, and especially culture. We are good friends with the royal family of Puri Ubud, especially with Tjok 'De, whose full name is Drs. Tjokorda Gde Raka Sukawati, MM. Tjok 'De is one of the sons of the late King of Ubud, Tjokorda Gde Agung Sukawati. He is Managing Director of the Pita Maha Hotel Group (Hotel Tjampuhan, Hotel Pita Maha, and Hotel Royal Pita Maha) in Ubud, though he delegates the day-to-day management of the hotels to his staff.

Within the community of Ubud, Tjok 'De serves as Deputy Head of the Traditional Community, or *Wakil Bendesa*. He is also a lecturer in Marketing at Udayana University, where he teaches twice a week.

His eldest brother, Tjok Putra, whose full name is Drs. Tjokorda Gde Putra Sukawati, is *Penggelisir*, the acknowledged head of the royal family of Puri Ubud. He became Penggelisir to replace his cousin Tjokorda Gde Agung Suyasa, who passed away on 28 March 2008 and was honored with the great Pelebon on 15 July 2008. Tjok Putra is also Chairman of Museum Puri Lukisan, Head of the Advisory Board of the Bali Tourism Board, Head of the Ubud Community Council, and President Director of the Pita Maha Hotel Group. Whenever prominent visitors come to Ubud, Tjok Putra is usually the first person to greet them.

The second oldest brother in the family is Tjok Ace, whose full name is Dr. Ir. Tjokorda Gde Oka Artha Ardana (AA) Sukawati, M.Si. He is currently serving as Regent of Gianyar and Chairman of the Bali branch of the Indonesian Hotel and Restaurant Association (PHRI). Like Tjok 'De, Tjok Putra also teaches at Udayana University, as a lecturer in architecture. He also holds a doctorate cum laude in Cultural Studies from Udayana University, which he earned in September 2008. Before becoming Regent, he was Deputy President Director of the Pita Maha Hotel Group.

Apart from these three brothers, another influential member of Puri Ubud is Tjokorda Raka Kerthyasa, S. Sos., M.Si., known as Tjok Ibah.

Tjok Ibah is a nephew of the last King of Ubud, Tjokorda Gde Agung Sukawati, and therefore a first cousin of Tjok Putra, Tjok Ace and Tjok 'De. Tjok Ibah owns and operates the Hotel Ibah. As well as serving as Chairman of the Bali Heritage Trust (Pelestarian Warisan Budaya Bali) and Head of the Traditional Community (*Bendesa*), he was recently elected to the Bali Provincial Legislature (DPRD) for the 2009-2014 term.

Because of this unique combination of positions—Bendesa of Ubud (head of the traditional community) and directly-elected popular representative in the provincial government—Tjok Ibah is simultaneously a traditional leader and a spokesman for the public within the formal government. In drafting regulations, for example, Tjok Ibah plays an active role in formulating *awig-awig* (traditional local regulations) with reference to the prevailing laws of the nation.

Another well-known figure from the Puri Ubud family is Dr. Ir. Tjokorda Raka Sukawati "Sosrobahu". Tjokorda "Sosrobahu" is an engineer who invented a hydraulic non-friction rotating device for road flyovers, one of Indonesia's most important technological achievements. This invention has been internationally recognized and is used not only in Indonesia but also abroad. Tjokorda "Sosrobahu" has proven that a native of Ubud can produce technological inventions that bring great benefits to society.

You have no doubt noticed that all their names are preceded by the title "Tjokorda". *Tjokorda* means "prince", indicating that they are members of a puri family. Another title that indicates the person is from a puri family is *Anak Agung*.

All these royal princes are talented artists as well. They possess knowledge and skills in the artistic and cultural realms and are always actively involved in the various traditional religious activities in Ubud. We have often seen them making barong, preparing for ceremonies, or discussing matters with the local community, with no social distance at all between them and the "commoners".

It is fair to call these princes the protectors and patrons of Ubud's society, who have enabled Ubud to maintain its culture and traditions while not neglecting the positive aspects of modern development.

To us, these princes personify Ubud as a whole. In their daily life, they are very friendly and eschew excessive luxury. Though they are respected community figures, you wouldn't know by looking at them that they come from a noble family. Aside from Tjok Ace, who as Regent of Gianyar is bound by a certain amount of protocol, you might see the princes anywhere around town. They dress the same as other local men, in a short-sleeved shirt, often with the top button undone, a headcloth (*udeng*), and a sarong. Only for special ceremonies do they dress more formally, mostly in white.

Like other people in Ubud, they enjoy chatting and swapping stories. And for some reason, every time we've just had a good chat with any of them, we feel refreshed and inspired. So we're always happy to spend time chatting with them.

We see for ourselves that Ubud has now entered a new era: Ubud 3.0. If the central roles in the Ubud 1.0 and Ubud 2.0 eras were played by Rsi Markandya and Tjokorda Gde Agung Sukawati, now in Ubud 3.0 the role of community leader and patron is being played collectively by the members of the Ubud royal family.

This new era, Ubud 3.0, is also characterized by rapid physical modernization and concurrent changes in community behavior. In this new era, Ubud is not only the cultural center of Bali but also a center for healing the human spirit, with many associated facilities and activities.

Figure 2.10 Tjok Putra, Tjok Ace, and Tjok 'De (from left to right; courtesy of Puri Ubud)

Figure 2.11 Tjok Putra (left, white shirt with black eyeglasses) and Tjok Ibah (center, black shirt) overseeing Pelebon ceremony (courtesy of Puri Ubud)

Figure 2.12 Tjok Ace welcoming Indonesian President, Mr. Susilo Bambang Yudhoyono, and Mrs. Ani Yudhoyono at Puri Ubud (courtesy of Puri Ubud)

Figure 2.13 Tjok Ace after Calon Arang performance (courtesy of Puri Ubud)

Figure 2.14 Tjok 'De overseeing Barong blessing ceremony (courtesy of Puri Ubud)

Figure 2.15 Tjok 'De constructing bade (cremation tower) for Pelebon ceremony (courtesy of Puri Ubud)

Tourism Activities in Puri Ubud

Facilities owned and operated by the Puri Ubud family have contributed greatly to Ubud's cultural development. Puri Ubud, also called Puri Saren Ubud, has a strong tradition of social and community welfare that includes helping with the repair and renovation of temples throughout the Ubud area. Puri Ubud also coordinates the traditional religious activities at temples in several neighboring villages.

The buildings of Puri Ubud, the official residence of the royal family, are in traditional Balinese architectural style and have been well maintained for centuries. Made of red brick, they are decorated with typical Balinese carvings and statues, both wooden and stone, in various corners and other places. The statues are dressed in Balinese sarongs with black, white and red checkered patterns. In addition to statues, many large ceramic pots, barong, and gamelan instruments are kept in the palace complex, which is roofed in black thatch (*ijuk*) from sugar palm fibers.

Every evening at 7.30, the open courtyard of Puri Ubud is the venue for cultural performances. It's always full of visitors, at least a hundred or so. The Puri Ubud courtyard is spacious, shaded, and paved with concrete blocks, making it a comfortable place for tourists to relax and enjoy the show.

Figure 2.16 Puri Ubud in recent times

Puri Ubud is not the only venue for cultural performances. Just a hundred meters west of Puri Ubud, Pura Taman Kemuda Saraswati, also known as the Ubud Water Palace, holds dance performances every Thursday evening. The performances here have a different atmosphere from those at Puri Ubud, as they take place on a stage in the middle of a large pond full of floating lotus flowers. This temple, designed by the great Balinese artist I Gusti Nyoman Lempad, was named Saraswati in honor of Dewi Saraswati, the goddess of knowledge and arts.

Figure 2.17 Ubud Water Palace

Apart from these two venues, traditional cultural performances are held nearly every night at many other places in Ubud—temples, *bale banjar*, or museums. The dancers, musicians and crew at these performances come from the local community. Local teenagers also sell tickets to these performances, helping to stimulate Ubud's economy.

And as well as traditional Balinese arts, there are sometimes performances of contemporary arts. For example, on 26 and 27 June 2009, there was a performance of a cross-cultural opera, "A House in Bali", directed by Evan Ziporyn. Inspired by the books and music of Colin McPhee, this work combines Western music with Balinese gamelan. McPhee was a Canadian musicologist and composer who lived in Bali in the 1930s. Ziporyn is a musician and music professor at the Massachusetts Institute of Technology (MIT), who studies and teaches traditional and modern Balinese music.

Figure 2.18 "A House in Bali" performance at Ubud Water Palace

Once again, we see how receptive Ubud's society is to positive influences from outside the traditional culture.

The community of Ubud, with its deep values of social solidarity and mutual self-help, regularly meets at the *wantilan* (village hall) directly opposite Puri Ubud to discuss various community affairs. Since the meeting place is so near the palace, the royal family learns immediately about any problems emerging in the community.

The wantilan is also the alternative venue, in case of rain, for the performances normally held at Puri Ubud. When it's not being used for community meetings or cultural performances, the wantilan serves as a place for people to hang out and relax, and as a convenient, strategically-located meeting point.

Banners are often posted outside the wantilan to announce current or coming activities in and around Ubud. Bazaars are also held here; for example, there's a charity bazaar at the end of the year, and New Year's Eve celebrations are held here.

Figure 2.19 The Wantilan

New Year's Eve in Ubud

On New Year's Eve (in the Western calendar) a bazaar is held in and around the wantilan. Small tents serving food are set up in the road. The organizing committee, comprised of people from the local community, roasts great quantities of pork and chicken. Other snacks and drinks are also sold for everyone's enjoyment.

At this event, people from the local community mingle freely with any tourists who happen to be in town. Everyone, wherever they're from and whatever their social status, is welcome to enjoy the food that is served.

Things get livelier around 10 PM. In addition to the food and drinks bazaar, the local banjar put on performances. They bring their gamelan instruments and play them while dancing in the streets. They take turns performing; each banjar tries to outdo the others. Each banjar plays in its own style, and tourists are urged to join the dancing.

The entire Puri Ubud family also attends this exciting event, which ends with a modest display of fireworks.

This is an interesting example of cultural innovation and collaboration. The content of the New Year's Eve celebration remains essentially Balinese, but it's served up in a modern package. The Balinese essence can be seen in the authentic cultural performances by the various banjar, while the modern aspect is evident from the use of modern instruments such as trumpets and the small-scale fireworks display.

Yet again, this shows how the people of Ubud are able to prudently blend their local values with positive outside influences. New Year's Eve parties are part of Western culture, but they have become a local tradition in Ubud. And the celebration is another manifestation of the social solidarity and mutual self-help inherent in Balinese society, because everything is arranged by the local community on an entirely voluntary basis.

Figure 2.20 New Year's Eve Celebration in Ubud

From the stories above, we see the important role played by the leaders of Ubud, from its founding to the present day. Rsi Markandya laid down the basic spiritual values of the community. The last King of Ubud, Tjokorda Gde Agung Sukawati, opened Ubud up to the outside world, while still protecting its cultural values. And his descendants continue this effort. Puri Ubud, the palace, is more than just a historical monument or a cultural symbol; its family plays an active role in the daily life of the community.

This is what gives Ubud its intense taksu, and why it makes such an impression on so many people. Ubud keeps up with the changing times, yet without losing its essential character. Its surface may change, but its spirit remains the same. And this spirit is hard to find anywhere else, even in other towns and villages in Bali.

(Endnotes)

1   This story of the history of Bali comes from http://indonesia-tourism.com/bali/history.html.

2   This story of Rsi Markandya is taken from several sources: First, an article entitled "Bersama Puri Membangun Ubud: Menciptakan Manusia Cerdas, Berilmu, dan Bertakwa" ("Together with the Palace, Building Ubud: Creating an Intelligent, Knowledgeable and Pious People") by Tjokorda Gde Agung Suyasa in the book *Kembang Rampai Desa Ubud* (*Anthology on the Village of Ubud*, Pustaka Nayottama, 2006). The secondary sources are a brochure from the Hotel Royal Pita Maha, which quotes the transcript of the Markandya Purana in the collection of Kesari Sanggraha, the book *Bali: Temple Festival* by Jane Belo (1996), and the book *Cult and Customs* by Dr. R. Goris and Drs. P.L. Dronkers. These sources were supplemented by several interviews with Drs. Tjokorda Gde Raka Sukawati, MM (Tjok 'De).

3   It is not entirely clear when Rsi Markandya arrived in Bali. Other sources say that he arrived in the 8th or the 10th century of the Christian era. Our reference to his arrival in the 11th century is based on the article by Tjokorda Gde Agung Suyasa mentioned in the preceding footnote.

4   This story of the role of the King of Ubud and his family is taken mostly from several interviews with Drs. Tjokorda Gde Putra Sukawati (Tjok Putra) and Drs. Tjokorda Gde Raka Sukawati, MM (Tjok 'De), as well as various other sources.

Chapter 3

Home of the Legendary Artists

"The painters of Ubud are able to transform what is in their imaginations into paintings without needing models... this indicates that the people of the village of Ubud are excellent artistic observers, as they are themselves a part of this art."

Arie Smit

Ubud's history and development cannot be divorced from the role played by the artists of Ubud, both locals and expatriates. As explained in the previous chapter, these artists and their works helped introduce Ubud to the outside world.

During the 1920s and 1930s, Ubud was already known as a center of Bali's arts community. One important impetus for the development of painting in Bali was the arrival of two European artists, Walter Spies (from Germany) and Rudolf Bonnet (from the Netherlands).[1]

Walter Spies was one of the first expatriates to live in Ubud. He initiated the establishment of the community of artists in Ubud, one of the most influential artists' communities in the world in the early 20th century.

Spies, born in 1895, was the son of a German diplomat and had lived in Russia and the Netherlands before coming to the Netherlands East Indies (now Indonesia). Arriving in Indonesia, Spies first lived in Yogyakarta as a painter and musician. In 1927, on the invitation of Tjokorda Gde Raka Sukawati, he moved to Ubud. At first, he stayed in the palace, Puri Ubud. Later, Spies built his own house, which is now the Hotel Tjampuhan.

Spies died in 1942, during the Second World War, when the ship taking him to Ceylon was bombed by the Japanese and sank.

Figure 3.1 Walter Spies (courtesy of Museum ARMA, from Horst Jordt, President of Walter Spies Foundation)

Another painter, Rudolf Bonnet, whose full name was Johan Rudolf Bonnet, was born in Amsterdam in 1895. Bonnet came to Bali on the suggestion of another Dutch painter, W.O.J. Nieuwenkamp, whom he met in Rome. Bonnet lived in Italy for eight years before coming to Bali; Nieuwenkamp had been to Bali in 1906.

Bonnet arrived in Bali in 1929 and immediately moved to Ubud. Bonnet was held as a prisoner of war by the Japanese during World War II. He left Bali in 1957 after refusing to sell a painting to President Soekarno, but he returned to Bali around 15 years later. Bonnet died in the Netherlands in 1978. Interestingly, he died at almost the same time as the King of Ubud, Tjokorda Gde Agung Sukawati, and the great maestro of Balinese art, I Gusti Nyoman Lempad.

Figure 3.2 Rudolf Bonnet (courtesy of Museum Puri Lukisan)

In Ubud, Spies and Bonnet became closely involved with local artists, especially painters and sculptors. Spies and Bonnet often visited painters in their homes to watch them at work. Bonnet also spoke Indonesian, which made it easier to communicate with the local artists.

These two artists introduced Western painting techniques, each in his own style. While Spies emphasized the play of light and shadows, color, and perspective in his works, Bonnet focused more on the anatomy of the body and human faces. Spies' works tended to be surrealistic, with dark colors, while Bonnet's were more realistic, mostly in black and white.

Figure 3.3 Walter Spies' works at Museum ARMA

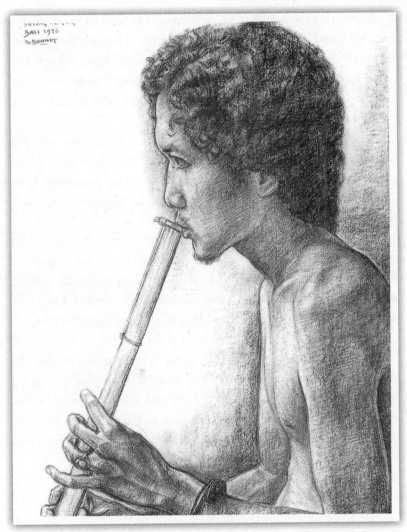

Figure 3.4 Rudolf Bonnet's works at Museum ARMA and Museum Neka

Spies and Bonnet recognized the extraordinary talent of Ubud's painters. But the painters themselves were unaware of their talent; they perceived painting not as a profession to earn money, but rather as a form of devotion to God (in the form of paintings and carvings for the temples) and as a sideline to their other work, mostly farming. They painted with no thought of selling their works.

Therefore, as well as sharing their experience with painting techniques, Spies and Bonnet slowly inculcated in the Balinese artists the idea that their paintings could be sold, and this would bring them much better incomes than they earned from farming. And as more tourists came to Ubud, "artist" came to be a recognized profession, because the Western tourists appreciated good art works.

But eventually this enthusiasm swung to the other extreme: with the increasing demand from tourists, some artists became interested only in producing as many works as possible, with no regard for quality. Spies and Bonnet were worried by this trend; they feared that if it persisted, the image and reputation of Ubud and its artists would be destroyed.

Spies and Bonnet therefore perceived the need to establish an association of Balinese artists to protect the quality of their work. They met with the King of Ubud, Tjokorda Gde Agung Sukawati, and his elder brother, Tjokorda Gde Raka Sukawati, and eventually, together with Bali's most renowned artist of the time, I Gusti Nyoman Lempad, they founded an association called "Pita Maha" in 1936.[2]

There's an interesting lesson to be drawn here. Spies and Bonnet had absorbed the spirit and values of Ubud; when Ubud's own artists started to pursue something that deviated from that spirit, it was these two expatriates who took steps to set them back on the right path. Precisely because so many individuals have worked to protect it, the spirit and values of Ubud have remained strong to this day.

Pita Maha: The Artists' Association

The founding of Pita Maha was a milestone in the development of art, not just for Ubud or Bali but for Indonesia and indeed the world. The name Pita Maha means "Great Shining".

The members of this association of artists from in and around Ubud made a commitment: their works would only be sold in the market after being approved by Pita Maha's team of experts. Pita Maha also worked to introduce the works of Ubud's artists more widely, through shows in Indonesia and abroad. Pita Maha was truly a pioneer in establishing a network among the artistic communities of Bali, Indonesia, and the world.

It was then that the community of Bali started to recognize the appreciation that their creative works, such as paintings and carvings, were receiving. Their creativity enabled Balinese artists to produce works with far greater artistic value than others might have created using the same materials.

Among the Balinese artists who joined Pita Maha were I Gusti Nyoman Lempad, Anak Agung Gde Sobrat, Ida Bagus Made Poleng, I Gusti Ketut Kobot, Ida Bagus Made Togog, and I Gusti Made Deblog. This community of artists first met at a guest house belonging to the royal house of Ubud.

In terms of themes, styles, and painting materials, the establishment of Pita Maha led to several fundamental changes. The themes explored by Bali's artists became more varied. Previously, most paintings dealt with stories from the Ramayana, Mahabharata and Bharatayuda epics, or with Balinese folk tales. And the style was also fairly standard, resembling wayang figures. Most materials were taken from natural sources, such as plants, soil, or animal bones, and small strips of bamboo were used as brushes.

Under the influence of Spies and Bonnet, the themes of Balinese paintings started to venture into scenes of daily life in rural Bali, such as farmers working in the rice fields, traders in the market, and of course ceremonies in the temples.

In line with this expansion of themes, the style of the paintings was no longer restricted to wayang-like forms; each painter was free to explore his own personal style. Painters also began to use modern painting materials—watercolors, oils, canvas, and paintbrushes.

Individual painting styles began to emerge, making it easier to recognize the works of a particular artist. Previously, it was difficult to identify the artist of any given work, since most artists had very similar styles; often, indeed, they worked anonymously, not signing their works.

Figure 3.5 An anonymous painting of Kamasan style (courtesy of Museum ARMA)

Figure 3.6 Anak Agung Gde Sobrat's work, one of Pita Maha artists (courtesy of Museum Neka)

From the perspective of marketing, this means that the painters, unconsciously, were starting to establish product differentiation, with their own individual artistic personalities. People could more easily tell one artist's works from another's. And because each artist maintained a fairly consistent style, they established definite characters and reputations.

Pita Maha's activities ended with the outbreak of the Second World War; Walter Spies was killed, and Rudolf Bonnet was a prisoner of war. The spirit of Pita Maha only reemerged in the 1950s with the establishment of the Museum Puri Lukisan.

Antonio Blanco: The Eccentric Maestro

As well as Walter Spies and Rudolf Bonnet, another painter who helped make Ubud famous was Antonio Blanco.

Antonio Blanco, a descendant of Spaniards, was born in Manila in 1911. He came to Singaraja, North Bali in 1952 after reading a book by the Mexican painter Miguel Covarrubias, *Island of Bali,* which was published in the 1930s. Covarrubias's descriptions of Bali as an island of heavenly beauty captivated Blanco; he had to come to Bali.

Singaraja was Blanco's first stop, as it was Bali's largest city at the time. But he was disappointed; he didn't find his "heaven" in Singaraja, since it was quite dirty in those days. Tjokorda Gde Agung Sukawati, the King of Ubud, then invited Blanco to come to Ubud; Blanco was even given two hectares of land to live on.

This maestro, who always wore a red beret, deeply loved Bali, and he also deeply loved his Balinese wife, Nyi Ronji, who was 24 years younger than him. He first met her when she brought him his meals of rice and vegetables while he was painting. Nyi Ronji, a dancer, later became Blanco's wife and the model for many of his paintings.

Antonio Blanco was famous for his eccentricities. Once when he was painting, some cows passed by, and the sound of their bells bothered him; it broke his mood, he couldn't paint with all that racket. He asked his wife to chase the cows away. She ended up giving the cowherd some money to take them elsewhere.

And once when someone wanted to buy a painting from him, Blanco was so busy shouting for hot coffee that the customer gave up and abandoned the purchase. Another time, when someone asked the price of a painting, he was abruptly shown the door, accused of not "respecting" the work, even though Blanco really needed the money.

Antonio Blanco never had a gallery anywhere other than Bali. He was awarded the highest noble title of "Don" by King Juan Carlos of Spain, an honor also accorded to another legendary Spanish painter, Salvador Dali. Because of these similarities—both personally eccentric, and both holding the title "Don"—Antonio Blanco was sometimes called the "Dali of Bali".

Blanco's paintings were unusual; nearly all portrayed nude women. It was said he'd been in his mother's womb for eleven months; that's why he loved women's bodies so much. And in his early days in Bali, many women still went bare-breasted; this inspired his paintings as well.

There's a story that accompanies one of his paintings, "The Meaning of Life (Mystic - Erotica)". Antonio Blanco was asked by an art collector from London, "Antonio, you are rather philosophical; what have you found to be the meaning of life?" Antonio replied, "When I am biting into a ripe succulent mango in my right hand, and at the same time fondling (with my left hand) the firm buttocks of an 18-year-old girl…..er…..Model, THAT I have found to be the closest THING to a MEANING FOR LIFE."

Interesting, eh? Antonio Blanco certainly loved women, and he poured his entire soul and all his feelings into his canvases. But he was also quite philosophical and humorous.

Antonio Blanco once said, "I cannot live without women." But he was no Don Juan; nearly all his paintings were inspired by his beloved wife, Nyi Ronji.

And though he had no students—unlike Walter Spies and Rudolf Bonnet, who taught painting—and never joined the Pita Maha group, his works became famous. Blanco became a great artist whose fame helped develop Ubud. And so when he died in 1999, even though he was not a Hindu, with the approval of the royal family of Ubud a *pelebon* or *ngaben* was held to cremate Blanco's remains.

Antonio Blanco was a Catholic, and there was no Catholic church in Ubud. Once when his son, Mario Blanco, asked him how he wanted to be buried, Antonio Blanco simply answered, "I will live until 100 years."[3]

Figure 3.7 Don Antonio Blanco with his wife, Nyi Ronji (courtesy of Museum Blanco)

Figure 3.8 Don Antonio Blanco's works (courtesy of Museum Blanco)

Arie Smit: The Second Milestone

If Walter Spies and Rudolf Bonnet, with their Pita Maha association, set the first milestone for the development of painting in Ubud, then the arrival of Arie Smit can be considered the second such milestone, giving rise to a new generation of painters in Ubud.

Arie Smit was born Adrianus Wihelmus Smit in 1916 in Zaandam, the Netherlands. Smit was sent to the Netherlands East Indies (Indonesia) for his military service in 1938. He worked as a lithographer for the Dutch military Topographical Service in Batavia, producing maps of the East Indies.

With the outbreak of World War II in the Asia-Pacific in 1942, Smit was captured by the Japanese. He spent over three years at hard labor with other prisoners of war, building roads, bridges and railroads in Singapore, Thailand, and Burma.

When the war ended in 1945, Smit was freed, and he returned to Indonesia. He became an Indonesian citizen in 1951 and taught graphic arts and lithography at the Bandung Institute of Technology (ITB).

In 1956, Smit visited Bali for the first time, and fell in love with the place immediately. After staying for two months, he decided to move to Bali.

In the early 1960s, Smit started providing artistic guidance to teenagers in Penestanan village, Ubud. They met each week under Smit's supervision, were given paper and paints, and were allowed to paint whatever they wanted. This gave rise to a naïve, colorful painting style, resembling children's paintings but with stronger composition, allowing the objects in the paintings to be recognized. This came to be known as the "Young Artist" style.

Smit's own painting methods were quite unusual. He never painted directly at the location of the subject of this painting; he made sketches, and then completed the work in his studio.

At the time of this writing, Arie Smit is still alive. Over 90 years old, he lives in a villa owned by Suteja Neka. In recognition of his role in developing the art of painting in Bali, in 1992 the Bali Provincial Government granted Smit the Dharma Kusuma award and a gold medal.[4]

Figure 3.9 Arie Smit (right) and Suteja Neka (courtesy of Museum Neka)

Figure 3.10 Arie Smit's works (courtesy of Museum Neka)

Lempad: The Balinese Grand Master

It was not only Western expatriates that played an important role in developing art in Ubud; Balinese artists played an equally important role. Of the many great artists of Bali, one has become a legend: I Gusti Nyoman Lempad.

Lempad, born in Bedulu village, Gianyar, in 1862, played a critical part in the development of art in Ubud. Lempad's home was always the first destination of expatriate artists and anthropologists such as Walter Spies, Rudolf Bonnet, Margaret Mead, Colin McPhee and Gregory Bateson in the 1920s and 1930s.

According to an interview with Lempad's son, I Gusti Made Simung, better known as Gusti Pekak, published in the magazine *Bali Echo*, the Lempad family lived in Blahbatu, near Gianyar, in the late 19th century; Lempad was a court artist at Puri Blahbatu.

Though Lempad later became best known as a painter, he was known earlier as an architect (in Balinese, *unagi*) and a highly skilled wood carver. It was Lempad that the King of Blahbatu turned to whenever he wanted to build a new temple or palace.

But one day Lempad and the King of Blahbatu had a serious disagreement, provoking the King's wrath. The kings in Bali exercised tremendous power in those days. For this supposed misdeed, Lempad was sentenced to a very severe punishment.

Fearing for his life, in around 1885 Lempad and his family moved to Ubud. Here he came under the protection of Ida Tjokorda Gde Sukawati, the King of Ubud at the time. Lempad and his family were later given some land to live on.

And from then on, Lempad was a court artist for the royal house of Ubud. He helped design and build Puri Ubud, and carved many of the statues still seen there. Lempad also designed and built Pura Taman Kemuda Saraswati (the Ubud Water Palace) in 1951-1952. Many of the sculptures in Pura Taman Kemuda Saraswati and in the adjoining Puri Sukawati are Lempad's works.

These works of Lempad's can still be seen in the Ubud area, but many of his earlier works were destroyed in the great earthquake of

1917. Lempad also made many barong and was renowned as an expert in the construction of *bade* (cremation towers).

And yet, because he had been working as an artist long before the Western artists came and influenced the local art scene, Lempad's paintings show no Western influence. His paintings are in a simplistic style: white backgrounds with images of people or figures resembling wayang kulit, and highly detailed. This style strongly resembles the traditional paintings on amulets and burial cloths, and the illustrations in lontar manuscripts. Most of the themes in his paintings derived from the Ramayana and Mahabharata epics or from Balinese folktales, occasionally with erotic and humorous elements.

Lempad first interacted with Western artists in around 1925. Later, in 1936, Lempad was one of the founders of Pita Maha. And when the Museum Puri Lukisan was established in the 1950s, Lempad was one of the first to donate his works to the museum's collection.

Lempad's works became famous in Europe and North America. In 1970, Lempad received an award from the Indonesian government in connection with the 25th anniversary of Indonesia's proclamation of independence. Lempad was also visited by US Apollo XVII astronaut, Ron Evans.

The story of Lempad's life was even made into a movie entitled "Lempad," produced and directed by John Darling and Lorne Blair and released in the mid-1980s.

Lempad passed away at 8:30 AM on Tuesday, 25 April 1978, aged well over 100. He spent his last moments in a very spiritual atmosphere. The sun was at its closest point to Gunung Agung; the day he died coincided with the Panca Wali Krama ceremony at Pura Besakih, a great month-long ceremony performed only once every ten years.

On the day of his death, Lempad summoned his family and asked them to bathe his body and dress him in white clothing. He told them he was ready to die, and uttered his last words: "Now all my works can be considered finished." Throughout his life, Lempad always took the view that all his works were still unfinished, and for that reason, none were ever sold. After conveying this final message, Lempad breathed his last.[5]

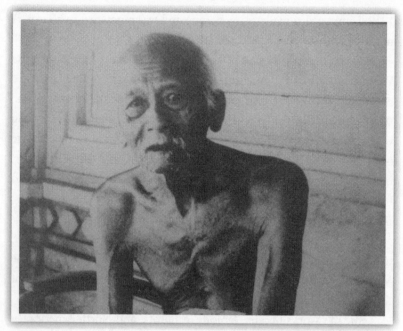

Figure 3.11 I Gusti Nyoman Lempad (courtesy of Museum Puri Lukisan)

Figure 3.12 Lempad's works (courtesy of Museum Puri Lukisan and Museum Neka)

From the stories of the great artists above, we see that it was their tremendous passion that made their works so monumental. They worked selflessly, with no ulterior motive (in Balinese, *ngayah*) for the interests of the temples and the palaces.

They had no commercial intentions when they produced their works. If some of their paintings later became expensive, they saw this mostly as a form of appreciation for the quality of the works, but this was never their primary motivation.

These artists also freely shared their knowledge with others, never worrying that someone else might imitate their painting techniques. Ultimately, this only enhanced their reputations, as they had many disciples who helped preserve the works of these legendary masters.

And to a great extent, the values prevailing in the local society influenced these artists as well. The people of Bali dedicate their entire lives to God. In the past, Balinese artists never signed their paintings, since they felt themselves to be merely the vehicles of the Gods. Many classic Balinese paintings are anonymous.

This only started to change when their works began to be purchased by Westerners, who wanted the painter's name on the painting. This Western influence was also felt in the performing arts. Before Western tourists came to Bali, the audience never applauded at the end of a performance; this habit was only adopted after tourists introduced the Western custom of clapping to express their appreciation.

The sincere dedication of performing artists, whether actors, dancers, or gamelan musicians, can still be seen today. Despite the very low pay—sometimes as little as Rp 10,000 (US$1) a night!—they display their skills with utmost devotion, as if they are playing for God, performing before God; they don't care how many people are in the audience. The audience we see may be small, but who knows how many from the hidden world might also be listening?[6] This is the kind of professionalism we see in Balinese artists. Even so, an enthusiastic audience still transmits positive energy to the performers.

For the Balinese, art is both a form of meditation and a cultural product. And the culture itself derives from spiritual values adapted to local conditions. This is why art, culture, and spirituality are inseparable.

Seen from a contemporary perspective, the great artists of the past were able to "find their own voice and inspire others to find theirs," to quote Stephen Covey in his book *The 8th Habit: From Effectiveness to Greatness.* Such people have been able to realize the essential meaning of their life in this world and to inspire others to find similar meaning for themselves.

These great artists played an important role and made invaluable contributions to the development of Ubud. Larger than life, they became demigods, deeply respected by the people of Ubud, and had many loyal disciples.

We also see that the local cultural environment played an important part in the development of great artists who came from outside Ubud. Feeling ill at ease in their places of origin, these artists moved to Ubud, which provided a more conducive environment for their artistic growth.

The community of Ubud, under the leadership of the King of Ubud, was receptive to the presence of these foreign artists because they were able to adopt the values, culture and lifestyle of the local community. Likewise, the people of Ubud learned from these artists and came to produce even more creative works; it was a mutually beneficial, symbiotic relationship. And eventually, these great artists became one with the local community, an inseparable part of Ubud.

This is an excellent illustration of how Marketing 3.0 has occurred in Ubud. When we work in alignment with the passion and spirit we find within ourselves, we become new persons, able to inspire those around us. And the legacy we leave behind us will live on, long after we are gone.

(Endnotes)

1   This story of Walter Spies and Rudolf Bonnet comes from several sources, including the book *Museum Puri Lukisan* written by Dr. Jean Couteau and published by Ratna Wartha Foundation (1999); the website of Gianyar Regency, http://www.gianyarkab.go.id; and the website "Walter Spies: His Life, His House in Bali", http://www.walterspies.com/walter_spies_biography.html.

2   The history of Pita Maha here is taken mostly from the book *Museum Puri Lukisan* by Dr. Jean Couteau.

3   The story of Antonio Blanco is taken primarily from the book *Fabulous Blanco* and interviews with Antonio Blanco's son, Mario Blanco.

4   The story of Arie Smit is based on information at the Arie Smit Pavilion in the Neka Art Museum (Museum Neka).

5   This story of the last moments of I Gusti Nyoman Lempad's life is based on information from a publication with unknown title and source seen in Lempad's house (Rumah Lempad) and from *Tempo* magazine, 10/VIII dated 6 May 1978.

6   The Hindu-Balinese recognize the existence of two worlds: Skala and Niskala. Skala is the tangible, physical world, while Niskala is the unseen world. These two worlds exist in parallel.

Chapter 4

Treasures in Museums

"If a museum is only a collection of art or its buildings, then it has no purpose. A museum is successful only if it provides a sense of history, development, and continuity."

Suteja Neka, founder of the Neka Art Museum

The word "museum" derives from the Greek *musea,* meaning "palace of the gods". A museum is a place where the best works of great artists are preserved and displayed. Through museums, the general public can enjoy these great works and learn about their history and background.

Imagine if there were no museums. These works would be kept in the homes of the artists, or of a handful of collectors, and the public would never be able to enjoy and appreciate them. And it is a great loss if people do not know the history of their civilization, which they can see through the works of their great artists.

This is why the founders and managers of museums play a role just as important as that of the artists themselves. They conserve and display art works professionally, so that the public can properly enjoy them. And museum operators often hold art exhibits at other venues, so that art works can be seen by an even broader public.

Museum operators are, naturally, art lovers. When they establish museums, the commercial aspect (profit) is not their main consideration. In Bali, museums have been established as a manifestation of their founders' personal visions to preserve the culture of Bali. This spirit has been intrinsic to the shaping of the spirit of Ubud as a whole.

The museums in Ubud are both cultural destinations and places of beauty. As well as holding vast collections of art works, the museum buildings are works of art in themselves. The museum complexes in Ubud are extensive and visually pleasing. We never get bored strolling through them and admiring the artists' works, for not only do we expand our knowledge, but we are physically and spiritually refreshed as well.

Ubud is full of large museums representing a full range of local works. In this chapter, we discuss Museum Puri Lukisan, Museum Blanco, Museum Rudana, Museum Neka, and Museum ARMA, as well as the home of the late I Gusti Nyoman Lempad, all of which are important cultural symbols in Ubud.[1]

Museum Puri Lukisan[2]

This museum, managed by the Ratna Wartha Foundation, was the first museum in Ubud and is one of the most important museums in Indonesia. It houses many historic works by the legendary artists of Ubud.

Museum Puri Lukisan, located on Jalan Raya Ubud, has a long and important history in the development of Ubud's art and culture. Its founding is closely associated with the institution called Pita Maha (see Chapter 3).

After founding Pita Maha in 1936, Tjokorda Gde Agung Sukawati, Walter Spies, and Rudolf Bonnet began to think about establishing a museum as a place to preserve and display the works of the Pita Maha artists. But because World War II broke out, and then the war for Indonesian independence, they were unable to follow through on this idea.

But once the situation was back to normal, the idea reemerged. Tjokorda Gde Agung Sukawati and Rudolf Bonnet became recommitted to the idea of founding a museum; Bonnet himself designed the building. The plans to establish the museum began with the formation of the Ratna Wartha Foundation on 1 October 1953 as the operator of the future museum. On 31 January 1954, the Prime Minister of the Republic of Indonesia, Ali Sastroamijoyo, laid the cornerstone, and finally in 1956 the museum was inaugurated by the Minister of Education, Instruction and Culture, Mr. Mohammad Yamin. Yamin gave the museum its name, Museum Puri Lukisan, the "Palace of Paintings".

Many parties contributed financially to the establishment of the museum, among them the national Department of Education, an association of Indonesians in London, a community group from Surinam, and international organizations such as Sticusa and the Ford Foundation.

The museum complex is extensive, comprising three buildings: a main building in the middle, with wings on the left and right. When it was opened, there was only the main building; the two wings were added in 1972.

The main building houses a permanent collection of classical Balinese paintings, including works by Lempad and by other Pita Maha artists. The front wall of the main building also displays carvings by Lempad. The wing on the left, Building II, displays modern traditional Balinese paintings by artists after the Pita Maha period, and the wing on the right, Building III, is usually used for exhibits of works by contemporary artists.

The courtyard within the museum is spacious, shady, and full of trees, with a large pool in the middle. At the entrance gate, there used to be a small bridge over the river; this has now been filled in to serve as a parking area, with a large entrance gate (in Balinese, called the *candi bentar*).

The museum has a very diverse collection. There are works by expatriate artists who lived in Ubud starting in the 1920s, such as Walter Spies and Rudolf Bonnet. There are also works by Bali's leading artists, such as Anak Agung Gde Sobrat, I Gusti Made Deblog, Ida Bagus Gelgel, and of course I Gusti Nyoman Lempad.

The range of works on display here shows us that traditional Balinese painting was never static; small changes were constantly taking place.

This indicates that Bali's artists are always receptive to changes that are in line with their culture and values.

Museum Puri Lukisan also hosts a wide range of educational activities, including lessons in painting, making wayang kulit, playing gamelan, kite making, mask making, wood carving, preparing Balinese offerings, basket weaving, flute playing, and dance.

So this museum is not just a place for passive tourism. Visitors can not only walk through and look at the paintings, but can also become actively involved by learning to paint or taking part in other artistic activities. Such experiences obviously leave tourists with a lasting impression; visitors to the museum can truly absorb the spirit of Ubud.

Figure 4.1 Museum Puri Lukisan

Figure 4.2 Wood carving workshop at Museum Puri Lukisan

Figure 4.3 Tjokorda Gde Putra Sukawati, Chairman of Museum Puri Lukisan

Museum Blanco[3]

This museum is also the former home of the artist, Antonio Blanco (see Chapter 3). Museum Blanco, or to use its full name, the Blanco Renaissance Museum, is located on Jalan Raya Sanggingan, on the left side if you're coming from Pasar Ubud. The Museum is easy to recognize, because out front there is a unique monument in the form of a round green stone inscribed "The Blanco Renaissance Museum: Mario Blanco, Don Antonio Blanco, His Life, His Works, His Dreams; The home, the studio, the galleries, the garden, the Balinese family, and the creative works of the artist".

This museum is large, situated on 20,000 square meters. The driveway is quite steep. The main entrance to the museum is circular; overhead is a delightful inscription, "Through these portals pass the most beautiful people in Bali!"

In one corner of the museum, we can see a number of woodcarving artists at work. In the courtyard next to the museum is a collection of beautiful, colorful birds: golden macaws, Bali starlings, and white cockatoos, living in Balinese fruit trees. Museum visitors often have their pictures taken with these tame birds.

The museum's main building is called "Blanco World", and indeed, once we enter the museum it is as if we are in another world—the world of Antonio Blanco. Unlike the other museums, this one has works by only one artist: Blanco. The architecture, too, was designed by Blanco, harmoniously blending Western and Balinese concepts. Inside the museum, Blanco's favorite Spanish songs are constantly played. And this three-story building has no windows, so we are truly isolated from the outside world.

The entrance to Blanco World is also quite unusual, in the form of a giant statue representing Antonio Blanco's signature, vertically folded in two. To the left and right of this statue are statues of crowned dragons, and directly in front of the gate is a pool with a fountain, symbolizing the sea where the dragons live.

The first and second floors of the museum display works by Blanco, mostly female nudes. This has occasionally caused some awkwardness when important persons have visited. The current President of the Republic of Indonesia, Susilo Bambang Yudhoyono (SBY), once came to Museum Blanco. When SBY visited, all the paintings showing the "forbidden" parts of the female anatomy were covered up with small cloths or otherwise concealed.

On the third floor, the highest, is a balcony that offers a spectacular view. The corners of the balcony are decorated with gold-colored statues of male and female Balinese dancers. There is also a statue of Dewi Saraswati, the goddess of arts and science, in the uppermost position.

Yet not all Blanco's paintings are of women. One of his works consists of bits of printed advertisements. Another work portrays various brands of bath soap—Camay, Asepso, Lux, Marbella, Citra, Lifebuoy, and Maaroh. Another painting, entitled "The Addict", is decorated with 20 cigarettes—the potent Dji Sam Soe brand of *kretek,* Indonesian clove-laced cigarettes. There's even a work portraying "ET", the extraterrestrial film character popular in the early '80s.

Antonio Blanco's paintings are truly unique, in that the frames for the paintings were designed by Blanco himself. Thus, the frame is an intrinsic part of each painting. The carvings in the frames are very ornate, and some are even adorned with scarf-like cloths or peacock feathers. And for some of the paintings, the descriptive notes go far beyond simply describing the paintings; many of them were written by Blanco as poems.

It's clear that Blanco was very creative. He was one of the pioneers in making the picture frame an inseparable part of the painting itself.

Some paintings include small paper cutouts of the silhouette of the island of Bali, as a kind of signature of Antonio Blanco. Other works portray foreign celebrities, including Mick Jagger and Michael Jackson, who visited Museum Blanco.

Initially, Museum Blanco was a gallery and studio, and not a formal museum. When Antonio Blanco died in 1998, the museum was not yet finished. The current museum was only completed about a year after he died.

Museum Blanco is now the home of Antonio Blanco's son, Mario Blanco. Like his father, Mario Blanco is also a painter. Mario Blanco taught himself to paint, because his father refused to teach him. Antonio Blanco wanted his second child to be a lawyer, a doctor, or an economist. "Don't be a painter," Antonio told his handsome son. But Mario's passion and talent led him inevitably to the world of art. Mario Blanco started teaching himself to paint at a very early age; the first exhibition of his works was in 1969, when he was only seven!

But unlike his father, though their styles are quite similar, Mario Blanco's paintings do not deal mostly with women's bodies, but rather with fruit, flowers, and water. These themes suggest a religious spirit, because all religions use these elements to bring people closer to God.

This is evidently due to the influence of Mario's mother, Nyi Ronji, and of the social environment in Ubud, where traditional religious ceremonies are constant events. The subjects of Mario Blanco's paintings are mostly the items and materials used in these rituals—flowers, fruit, bowls, teapots, bottles and so on.

Museum Blanco is a good example of how the community of Ubud is willing to accept a museum founded by an expatriate artist, which does not even display any works by indigenous Balinese artists. This is possible because Antonio Blanco and his family are considered part of Ubud's society, since they have lived there for decades—yet another example of how receptive the people of Ubud are to outside influences that are in harmony with their age-old cultural values.

Figure 4.4 Museum Blanco (courtesy of Museum Blanco)

Figure 4.5 Mario Blanco (courtesy of Museum Blanco)

Museum Rudana⁴

Museum Rudana, founded by Nyoman Rudana, is in Peliatan village, in the southern part of Ubud. Museum Rudana exhibits a highly diverse range of works by various artists—indigenous Balinese artists, expatriate artists resident in Bali, and artists from other regions of Indonesia—from the past up to the present. Museum Rudana was established to be a kind of Gallery of Indonesia.

Nyoman Rudana, born in 1948, is a well-known community figure in Ubud. He is often called "Senator Rudana" because he served as one of Bali's members in the Indonesian national House of Regional Representatives (DPD) for the 2004-2009 term.

Rudana's love for the art world began in the 1960s. In those days, he regularly visited Museum Puri Lukisan, the home of Antonio Blanco, and the homes of many other artists to look at the various art works. In 1974, Nyoman Rudana established the Rudana Painter Community in

Sanur. Then, in 1978, he founded the Rudana Fine Art Gallery on 900 square meters of land in Ubud.

In December 1990, construction of Museum Rudana began on a 2500-square-meter plot, near the site of the Rudana Fine Art Gallery. The Museum was inaugurated on 26 December 1995 by President Soeharto as part of the celebrations of the 50th anniversary of Indonesia's independence.

The museum buildings are designed on the basis of Hindu-Balinese philosophy. The first aspect of this philosophy is Tri Angga, whereby the museum building consists of three levels, representing the head, body, and feet. The second aspect is Tri Mandala, whereby the museum's space is divided into inner, middle, and outer realms.

The Museum is now managed by Nyoman Rudana's oldest son, Putu Supadma Rudana, who is usually called Putu Rudana. His warm smile and his physical appearance remind us a bit of Barack Obama.

In addition to running the museum, Putu Rudana is also one of the editors of the art and culture magazine *Musea*, published by the Bali Museum Association (Himusba), in which he is also Third Chairman. The First Chairman of Himusba is Nyoman Gunarsa, a leading Balinese artist.

Putu Rudana's vision is not simply to promote the Museum Rudana. He says that if the museums in Indonesia are to become world famous like the Louvre in Paris, all museum operators in Indonesia must unite—not just those in Bali, but throughout Indonesia. He calls this vision "Artistic Synergy to Build Indonesia"—a concept of arts and culture to unite the Indonesian people. Because of this vision, Joop Ave, former Indonesian Minister of Tourism, has called Putu Rudana "Mr. Synergy".

The museum's collection comprises over 400 paintings and other art works. These include works by leading Balinese artists such as Nyoman Gunarsa and Made Wianta, and works by other Indonesian maestros such as Srihadi Soedarsono, Affandi, and Basuki Abdullah. All these works were collected and personally chosen by Nyoman Rudana and his wife, Ni Wayan Olasthini, in the museum's early days, and Putu Rudana is now continuing this acquisition process.

As well as finished paintings, we can also observe painters at work. Some are still making sketches; others are coloring their paintings. All are sitting on the floor on woven mats.

The museum complex is large and comfortable. In the middle of the tidy rear courtyard are two elephant statues, flanking a statue of the Buddha. The museum complex adjoins green rice fields, with coconut trees off in the distance.

This museum was designed to be a kind of Ubud in miniature; it seeks to replicate the atmosphere of Ubud, with rice fields, Balinese architecture, painters at work, and so on. There's also a temple, on which the moss is left to grow, typifying the "spirit" or "soul" of Ubud.

One interesting thing in this museum, not found anywhere else, is what is called the "windows of leadership". It's quite simple; just vertical windows, not that large, running from the ground floor up to the top floor. Though it seems simple, it reflects a deeper philosophy.

As Nyoman Rudana explains, when we are on the ground floor and look out the windows, our outlook or horizon will lead us to look mostly at the things above. The sky dominates, taking up a greater proportion of the view than the panorama of the rice fields. This indicates that the followers—the lower classes, so to speak—will always look upward and seek guidance from their leaders.

But when we are on the top floor, the view of the rice field predominates; we don't see much of the sky. This means that a leader must always look downward; in other words, a true leader must know what is happening in his community.

An extraordinary philosophy, isn't it?

According to Putu Rudana, Indonesia's artistic and cultural heritage is truly our greatest asset. Our natural wealth may be depleted, since it is non-renewable. The value of technological equipment will also decline as time goes on, and most technology has very little local content anyway. But our cultural and artistic heritage is eternal, its value is always increasing, and the materials come from the natural environment.

Figure 4.6 Museum Rudana

Figure 4.7 "Windows of Leadership"

Figure 4.8 Putu Rudana (sitting) and Nyoman Rudana (right) with one of Indonesian maestro, Srihadi Soedarsono, and his work, Borobudur (courtesy of Museum Rudana)

Museum Neka[5]

Museum Neka, or the Neka Art Museum, was founded and is operated by Pande Wayan Suteja Neka. As stated on the plaque at its entrance, this museum, on Jalan Raya Sanggingan, was opened in 1976 and inaugurated in 1982 by the Minister of Education and Culture of the Republic of Indonesia, Dr. Daoed Joesoef.

The museum has a long and interesting history. Suteja Neka was a primary school teacher for ten years (1959-1969). In the mid-1960s, Suteja Neka, then only 27, became interested in pursuing a profession in the art world when he saw foreign tourists buying Balinese paintings.

So he decided to open an art gallery to sell his own works, the works of other local artists, and carvings by his father, I Wayan Neka, a renowned wood carver. The gallery, on Jalan Raya Ubud, was opened in 1966.

Suteja Neka's father, I Wayan Neka (1917-1980), was a very famous artist in his time. He received an award as Best Carver in the Province of Bali in 1960. He was also the first Balinese artist to make a three-meter-high Garuda statue for the 1964 New York World's Fair, and did so again for the Osaka Expo in 1970.

Suteja Neka then became interested in starting a museum, because he saw so many great art works from Bali, especially paintings, being taken home by foreign tourists. This bothered him, so he started to collect paintings by local artists. In 1975, Suteja Neka traveled to Europe with Rudolf Bonnet to visit and study the museums there. And a year later, Suteja Neka opened his own museum.

In the front veranda of the museum is a carving in mimosa wood, entitled Statue of the Garuda Bird, carved by Wayan Neka in 1972. This area also displays photos of the museum's inauguration, which was attended by one of Indonesia's great master artists, Affandi.

As we enter the museum, first we come to a number of classical and traditional Balinese paintings, including ones in the Kamasan, Ubud, and Batuan styles. Next we encounter paintings (originals or reproductions) by Walter Spies, Rudolf Bonnet, Arie Smit, Antonio Blanco, and Miguel Covarrubias. There are also works by well-known Balinese artists such as Ida Bagus Made Poleng and Ida Bagus Nyoman Rai.

We also see works that, while in traditional style, portray daily life in modern times, such as paintings by I Wayan Bendi and by I Made Budi portraying the atmosphere when President Soeharto and his wife visited Bali in 1987. Another section exhibits more contemporary paintings, though still with a Balinese flavor.

In another area, we find works by maestros from other regions of Indonesia, such as Fadjar Sidik, Widayat, Hendra Gunawan, Sindudarsono Sudjojono, and Dullah. There are also several masterpieces by Affandi, including self-portraits he made in 1975 and 1976.

One thing you won't find anywhere else is a special building dedicated to the works of Arie Smit and his students from Desa Penestanan, known as the Young Artists. Suteja Neka and Arie Smit are close friends. The

Arie Smit pavilion was officially opened on 3 September 1994, and Arie Smit lives in a villa owned by Suteja Neka.

There's also a Lempad Pavilion, dedicated to works of I Gusti Nyoman Lempad. Another building is the Photography Archive Center, containing black and white photos by Robert Koke, an American photographer who recorded his impressions of Bali in the 1930s and 1940s.

Yet another building is the Contemporary Indonesian Art Hall. To the left and right of the entrance to this two-story building are two statues of human figures, roughly one and a half times the height of a normal person. Amusingly, the faces of the statues somewhat resemble Suteja Neka's.

As well as displaying its permanent collection, Museum Neka also often shows works of young, contemporary artists from Bali and other regions.

The most unusual part of Museum Neka is the Keris Museum (the *keris* is the traditional dagger of Indonesia). Museum Keris was inaugurated at Museum Neka's 25th anniversary celebration by the Minister of Culture and Tourism, Jero Wacik, on 22 July 2007. Also present at the event was the Chairman of the National Heritage Board of Singapore, Prof. Dr. Tommy Koh. Suteja Neka is a member of the Singapore Art Museum Board and was appointed to the National Heritage Board of Singapore for the period 1 May 2006 to 31 July 2007.

The Keris Museum's collection comprises hundreds of keris, including heirloom keris from 18 kingdoms around the archipelago. The keris collection is very well organized; the keris are displayed in glass cases. Not just any keris can make its way into the museum's collection; the keris here have all been carefully selected by two Indonesian keris experts, Ir. Haryono Haryoguritno and KRAT Sukoyo Hadi Nagoro.

In addition to the many keris on display, the museum also offers literature relating to keris, including a book entitled *Pendekar-pendekar Besi Nusantara* (*Peasant Blacksmithing in Indonesia*) by S. Ann Dunham (Barack Obama's mother), and *Keris Jawa: Antara Mistik dan*

Nalar (Javanese Keris: Between Mysticism and Logic) by Ir. Haryono Haryoguritno.

Museum Neka may have the most complete keris museum in Indonesia. Suteja Neka himself is descended from keris makers; his first name is Pande, indicating a person from the blacksmith caste.

Museum Keris reminds us that art works in Bali are actually quite diverse. Most people know Bali for its paintings and wood carvings, but there are many other art media and formats that are less well known. The Keris Museum within Museum Neka also indicates that Ubud has become a center of Indonesian culture, because the keris is actually best known in Java.

Figure 4.9 Museum Neka

Figure 4.10 Museum Keris

Figure 4.11 Pande Wayan Suteja Neka (courtesy of Museum Neka)

Museum ARMA[6]

The next well-known museum in Ubud is the Agung Rai Museum of Art (ARMA), often just called Museum ARMA. This museum, on Jalan Raya Pengosekan, was inaugurated by the Minister of Education and Culture, Prof. Dr. Ing. Wardiman Djojonegoro, on 9 June 1996, though the building had been standing since 1989.

The founder of this museum is Agung Rai, who was born on 17 July 1955 in Peliatan to a poor farming family. At first, Agung Rai wanted to become a painter, and he studied painting with two prominent artists, Anak Agung Gede Raka Turas and Nyoman Darmana. But he gradually realized that he lacked the talent to be a painter.

So Agung Rai changed direction and instead became an entrepreneur in the art sector. In 1968, he gathered a number of paintings from his teachers and his colleagues, and sold them to foreign tourists in Mas village, near his home in Peliatan. This business was reasonably successful, so Agung Rai thought about expanding the enterprise.

In those days, the Kuta area was already swarming with foreign tourists, so in 1973, Agung Rai started selling art in Kuta. Early each morning, he would drive his motorbike down to Kuta, carrying paintings and other art works. This was also when he started teaching himself English in the restaurants full of foreign tourists. With his entrepreneurial instincts, he expanded his networks, both with other art vendors and with foreign tourists.

Then, with the money he had accumulated, Agung Rai opened an inn at his home in Peliatan, where foreign tourists could stay and look at other paintings. Finally, on 1 January 1978, he opened the Agung Rai Fine Art Gallery, the forerunner of the present Museum ARMA.

The Museum ARMA complex, which covers seven hectares, has two main buildings: Bale Daja (the north building) and Bale Dauh (the south building). Bale Daja, with an area of 3300 square meters, displays traditional Balinese paintings, such as those in the Batuan style from the 1940s. Bale Dauh, 1200 square meters, exhibits works of modern artists from Indonesia and abroad. In all, the two buildings contain over 250 paintings in styles ranging from traditional to contemporary.

The collection here is highly varied. We can see works by Western expatriate painters who lived in Ubud, such as Rudolf Bonnet, Miguel Covarrubias, Walter Spies, Antonio Blanco, Theo Meier, Le Mayeur, and Arie Smit.

Walter Spies is particularly honored here, with a special room dedicated to his works. These include one work by Walter Spies that does not portray scenes from Bali, but rather a night market or carnival in Russia.

In addition to these works by Western artists, there are also works by I Gusti Nyoman Lempad and anonymous classical paintings by other Balinese artists. Museum ARMA also exhibits works by Indonesian maestros from outside Bali, such as Raden Saleh Syarif Bustaman, Affandi, R. Basuki Abdullah, Dullah, Popo Iskandar, Guruh Soekarnoputra, Hendra Gunawan, S. Sudjojono, Bagong Kussudiardja, I Nyoman Gunarsa, Jeihan, and many others.

As well as displaying its vast collection of art works, Museum ARMA also has an open-air stage, where dance performances are given every night: Legong Klasik, Legong Telek, Topeng Jimat, Barong and Keris dances, Wayang Orang Ramayana, and Kecak Rina performed in person by Nyoman Rina, one of Bali's most famous *kecak* dancers.[7]

Museum ARMA also stages a form of traditional wrestling called *mepantigan*. Mepantigan is performed in a muddy field at night by torchlight. This same rice field is also used for other arts performances. As well as providing an interesting spectacle for tourists, this is to honor Dewi Sri, the goddess of fertility. These performances are meant to foster a greater love for agriculture among the people of Ubud and thereby maintain Bali's agrarian culture.

Besides all these cultural performances, Museum ARMA also hosts lessons in painting, dance, gamelan, wood carving, and cooking, and instruction in the Balinese Hindu religion. The museum complex also houses the ARMA Resort, expanded from the inn Agung Rai originally opened.

Agung Rai's vision is to make Museum ARMA "a living museum". He wants the museum not only to display art works to be viewed passively, but also to contain living art—not just paintings and carvings, but also performances. The buildings, gardens, and the premises surrounding the museum are all part of this "living museum" concept.

As another manifestation of this vision, Museum ARMA is not devoted solely to art-related activities. It is often the venue for activities relating to other current issues, such as peace and the environment. Agung Rai is an advisor to the Bali Institute for Global Renewal, which held Global Healing Conferences in 2004 and 2006.

Figure 4.12 Museum ARMA

Figure 4.13 Walter Spies collection at Museum ARMA

Figure 4.14 The Open Stage at Museum ARMA

Figure 4.15 Agung Rai (courtesy of Museum ARMA)

Rumah Lempad[8]

Another historic venue in Ubud is the home of the late painter and sculptor I Gusti Nyoman Lempad, usually just called Rumah Lempad, on Jalan Raya Ubud just east of Puri Ubud.

This is not a museum; as its name suggests, it is a house, just like many other traditional Balinese houses. Lempad's children, grandchildren and descendants still live there. It's nothing fancy; it doesn't look like the former residence of one of Bali's greatest artists. Consequently, tourists who visit Ubud often miss it.

Inside the house are paintings and sculptures by Lempad, incorporated as part of the home's interior design, not displayed as in a museum. Among the statues are a male and female couple, and a statue of a mother and child.

At the entrance to Rumah Lempad, there's a statue of a flute player wearing a cloak, who strongly resembles the Pied Piper of Hamelin. It's possible that Lempad was inspired to create this work by some of the Western artists who often stayed at his home. Next to the piper are statues of two sleeping cattle.

Figure 4.16 Rumah Lempad

Lempad's home gives us an idea of the lifestyle of Bali's leading artists in the past. They lived quite simply, just like most other people. It's very clear that the works by these artists were intended as a form of devotion to God, and for no other purpose.

Figure 4.17 "The Pied Piper of Hamelin" at Rumah Lempad

In addition to the museums described above, Ubud is also full of galleries.[9] These galleries exhibit not only paintings and statues; there are also photo galleries, such as Galeri Rio Helmi on Jalan Suweta and Gambare Gallery on Jalan Raya Sayan.

It's fair to say that no visit to Ubud is complete if you haven't visited at least a few of these museums. In the museums, we can see hundreds—no, thousands—of masterpieces by great artists that can't be seen anywhere else. This is an excellent way to hone our emotional and spiritual intelligence.

And for those of us in the world of marketing, these museums give a meaningful inspiration.

In the field of marketing, one important concept is the "place" or "marketing channel" to display a product so that customers have easy access to it. Normally, a "place" is a shop where customers can see and buy a product.

Beyond this basic concept of "place", in the latest marketing concept called "New Wave Marketing", "place" has become what we call "Communal Activation". This means that the community is now able to replace the role of the store in marketing a given product.[10]

The role of the museums described above is quite similar to the role of "place" and "communal activation" in the world of marketing. Thanks to these museums, we can appreciate works by the legendary artists of the past. And the many activities conducted by the museums—both within the museums, and activities outside the museums, such as art exhibits—also foster a community of art lovers, who in turn promote these works of art.

Each of these museums, deliberately or not, also has what is known in marketing as its own positioning, and builds its differentiation based on that positioning.[11]

Museum Puri Lukisan was the first museum in Ubud and displays mostly works by artists of the Pita Maha generation. Museum Blanco was the home of Antonio Blanco, and displays only works by Antonio Blanco in its Blanco World. Museum Rudana is referred to as the "Gallery of Indonesia", because its collection is so diverse, and it also features the highly philosophical "Window of Leadership".

Museum Neka focuses on works by Lempad and Arie Smit, and is the only museum in Bali with a keris collection. And Museum ARMA has quite a complete collection of works by Walter Spies, and is known as the "living museum" for its many cultural performances.

Though all are under modern management, whereby each museum is run as a corporate entity, the museums in Ubud are not operated primarily for commercial purposes. These museums exist as a means to trace the development of art and culture in Ubud and the trends in creativity from past to present. Each museum was established because its founder had deeply artistic character and an intense passion for the arts.

We also see how the founders and operators of the museums design and maintain their buildings with utmost attention to the comfort of visitors and concern for the natural environment. Most of the museum buildings are in traditional Balinese architectural style, on extensive premises shaded with leafy trees. This is in line with the Tri Hita Karana philosophy of the people of Ubud.

Thus, the museums themselves are valuable works of art. Visitors can appreciate not only the art works a museum contains, but also the ambience of the museum itself.

(Endnotes)

1   The descriptions of the museums are based mostly on visits to the respective museums, supplemented by other sources as mentioned in each description.

2   This history and profile of Museum Puri Lukisan comes mostly from the book *Museum Puri Lukisan* by Dr. Jean Couteau.

3   This history and profile of Museum Blanco comes mostly from interviews with Mario Blanco, the book *Fabulous Blanco*, and the Museum Blanco website, http://www.museumblanco.com.

4   This history and profile of Museum Rudana comes mostly from interviews with Putu Supadma Rudana and Nyoman Rudana's website, http://www.senatorrudana.com.

5   This history and profile of Museum Neka comes mostly from interviews with Suteja Neka, the museum brochures, and the Museum Neka website, http://www.museumneka.com.

6   This history and profile of Museum ARMA comes mostly from the museum brochures and the Museum ARMA website, http://www.armamuseum.com.

7   *Tari Kecak* is a dance form that is very popular with tourists. The current form of the Tari Kecak was created by Walter Spies and a Balinese dancer named Limbak in the 1930s.

8   For the full story of I Gusti Nyoman Lempad, see Chapter 3.

9   A museum differs from a gallery. In a museum, most if not all of the works on display are original, classic works by leading artists; in contrast, a gallery generally displays reproductions of works by artists of the past or original works by newer artists.

10   For more on the concept of New Wave Marketing, see the book *New Wave Marketing*.

11   "Positioning" and "Differentiation" are two very popular concepts in marketing. Positioning is the perception we seek to create in the minds of consumers, while Differentiation is the actual manifestation of that Positioning.

Chapter 5
Religious and Spiritual Life

"I feel I was re-incarnated on this earth to create what the Gods direct... Most important are cremation towers that transport souls of the dead to the other world, and cremation bulls that make their journey a smooth one."
I Gusti Nyoman Lempad

It would be difficult to find another place on earth where the religious and spiritual atmosphere is as intense as it is in Bali, and especially in Ubud. This is evident from most aspects of life here, particularly in people's day-to-day behavior. The Hindu-Balinese are famous for being very spiritual and firm in upholding their customs and culture.

Perhaps only in Bali does the airport close for an entire day to celebrate a religious holiday. On Nyepi[1], 26 March 2009, Ngurah Rai International Airport was closed from 6 AM until 6 AM the following day. During these 24 hours, the 150 flights normally scheduled by 13 domestic and 19 international airlines were not allowed to land or to take off. As well as the airport, the seaports that provide the other main access to Bali were also closed.

The religious-spiritual atmosphere of Bali is also evident from the many *pura*, or temples, which are literally everywhere—from the small pura within homes for family rituals to the huge one used by the entire Hindu populace of Bali, called *kahyangan jagat*, or "the abode of the gods on earth": Pura Besakih. It's estimated that there are over 20,000 temples on Bali. This is why, as well as being known as "the island of Gods", Bali is also called "the island of a thousand temples".

The Hindu-Bali community's devotion to its religion and its customs can also be seen in the many religious ceremonies that take place. In every ceremony, we see the Balinese making offerings in the form of *canang* or *banten*.[2]

While banten are only offered at major ceremonies at the temples, you see canang every day and everywhere—in the streets, at the doors of villas, on statues, on car dashboards, even near a laptop where someone is working. These offerings are a symbol of thanks to God for the blessings that have been bestowed.

Figure 5.1 Canang offering at a temple

Another form of respect to God is shown by Balinese women when they carry banten; always on top of their heads, never in their hands, which would be easier. They place the banten on their heads, because the head is the holiest and highest part of the human body, and therefore the only appropriate place to carry such an offering to God.

Bali is indeed an Island of a Thousand Ceremonies. Some traditional religious ceremony takes place nearly every day, for one reason or another: smaller ceremonies for tooth filing, commemoration of the third month since the birth of a child, the rice planting process, building a house or temple, and the major ceremonies such as the Odalan (anniversary) of a large temple or the Pelebon (cremation) of an important community figure. It is estimated that the average Balinese woman spends around a third of her waking hours on activities related to these rituals!

Figure 5.2 A woman carrying banten

So when you are in Bali, and especially in Ubud, you're very likely to see at least one of these traditional religious ceremonies. Most of these ceremonies are not scheduled and therefore not mentioned in the tourist guidebooks. But if you're interested in seeing ceremonies, just ask the local people, and they'll be happy to tell you when and where they are being held.

As well as being a form of devotion and an expression of thanks to Almighty God, these numerous ceremonies also stimulate the local economy. Major events such as the great Pelebon or Ngaben in Ubud in mid 2008 can attract hundreds of thousands of visitors. So this is a clear manifestation of the Tri Hita Karana philosophy.

Major ceremonies are always held in temples. One historic temple in Ubud, and one of the oldest in Bali, is Pura Gunung Lebah.

Pura: The Centers of Devotion

The word *pura* derives from Sanskrit and means a space enclosed by walls. The word *pura* also comes from the same root as the word *puri*, or palace. So it's not surprising that the physical forms of pura and puri show many similarities, as do the roles and activities performed in these two places.

Each village has three main temples: the Pura Desa (the pura to worship Dewa Brahma, the Creator), the Pura Puseh (the pura to worship Dewa Wisnu, the Preserver), and the Pura Dalem (the pura to worship Dewa Siwa, the Destroyer). Together, these three pura are called *Kahyangan Tiga*, the abodes of the three gods. The family temples in homes are derivatives of these three pura. The Pura Desa is also often referred to as the *Bale Agung*, or Great Hall.

There are specific rules about pura construction. The Pura Desa is built in the middle of the village; the Pura Puseh is located in the direction *Kaja*, toward the mountains (in Ubud, to the north); and the Pura Dalem is located in the direction *Kelod*, toward the sea (in Ubud, to the south).

At the level of Bali as a whole, all three of these temples are contained within the Pura Besakih complex, often called the "Mother Temple" because the temple structures are enormous and situated on a vast plot of land. Major ceremonies are always held at Pura Besakih. Gunung Agung, the highest mountain in Bali, where Pura Besakih is located, is in fact part of a series of holy mountains, together with the Himalaya in India and Gunung Semeru in Java. These mountains on earth are considered a replica of Mahameru, the mountains in *swah loka* (heaven).

In the Ubud area, Pura Desa Ubud is on Jalan Raya Ubud, near Jalan Kajeng; Pura Puseh Ubud is on Jalan Suweta, north of Puri Ubud (the Palace); and Pura Dalem Ubud is on Jalan Raya Ubud, west of Pura Desa. These temples serve not only as places of worship to the almighty gods, but also as places to foster good relations among the villagers.

Apart from these three main pura, there are several other temples in Ubud, including Pura Taman Kemuda Saraswati (also known as the Ubud Water Palace). This pura is dedicated to Dewi Saraswati, the goddess of sciences and arts. Dewi Saraswati is also the consort of Dewa Brahma.

Ubud also contains another historic pura of great importance not only to the people of Ubud but to the community of Bali as a whole: Pura Gunung Lebah.

Figure 5.3 Pura Gunung Lebah

Pura Gunung Lebah, whose name means "temple situated in a mountain valley", is the main temple in Ubud. This pura symbolizes the stopping place of the founder of the village, Rsi Markandya, and lies at the confluence of two branches of the Oos River, which is a holy place for the Hindu-Balinese. From this temple, we can see the Ubud Bridge over the Oos, which connects Jalan Raya Ubud and Jalan Raya Sanggingan.

Pura Gunung Lebah, which is also an irrigation temple, stands near the Hotel Tjampuhan and the Hotel Ibah. You can reach the pura on foot or by motor vehicle on a rather steep downhill trail next to the Hotel Ibah. It's not far from the main road, only around 50 meters. Motor vehicles can park along Jalan Raya Sanggingan or in the parking lot of Kerta Yoga junior high school, right across from Pura Gunung Lebah.

Within the temple complex, which was the subject of paintings by the Indonesian maestro Affandi, is a statue of Rsi Markandya, the holy man who founded Ubud, as well as several structures including *meru*[3] and the *bale kulkul*[4].

Pura Gunung Lebah was the venue for the major Karya Agung Penyegjeg Bhumi ceremony held in October 1991. This ceremony, held once every hundred years, is aimed at purifying and protecting the surrounding natural environment. Inside the temple is a plaque commemorating this event, signed by Prof. Dr. Ida Bagus Oka, the Governor of Bali at the time.

The Pura Gunung Lebah complex consists of three areas: Nista Mandala, Madya Mandala, and Utama Mandala, collectively referred to as Tri Mandala. Nista Mandala is the outer area, located in the Kelod direction (closest to the sea, to the south). Madya Mandala is the middle area; and Utama Mandala is the holiest area, located in the Kaja direction (toward the mountains, to the north). This division of space based on the Tri Mandala concept is always employed by the Hindu-Bali community in spatial arrangements, especially for homes and temples.

Various traditional religious ceremonies are held at Pura Gunung Lebah. The preparation for, and the execution of, these ceremonies is an important part of local life, strengthening the bonds of social solidarity among all the community's members.

According to Tjok Putra and Tjok 'De, such activities are basically organizational activities. Just as in a company, if the cooperation between the leaders and the staff is effective, the aura will be positive and the results will be favorable. Conversely, if the cooperation is poor, the aura will also be poor, leading to an unfavorable result.[5]

This shows that the sense of social solidarity in Ubud remains very strong. Ubud's society is highly communal. All the activities undertaken are communal efforts, not those of individuals; each person is considered an inseparable part of a larger community, whether at the family level or the village level. This sense of community has been a critical factor in Ubud's development and has helped Ubud to sustain its spiritual and cultural values.

The Banjar: A Community of Values

In Balinese society, one important element of traditional community organization is the *banjar,* one level below the village or subdistrict administration. Each traditional village normally has between five and fifteen banjar. Although different banjar resemble each other in many respects, each banjar has its own unique character, in line with the changes that occur within the banjar.

The banjar's members are all married men. They are members not as individuals, but as the heads of their respective households; in this capacity, they are called *krama.* The other family members are thus automatically included as members of the banjar.

The banjar is further divided into smaller groups, called *tempek* and *sekaa.* A tempek is a group of banjar members who live near one another. The tempek usually manages any work that needs to be done collectively and is also a medium for dissemination of information. A sekaa is a small group that is formed on a voluntary basis, usually in connection with some artistic endeavor. The sekaa are the groups that normally put on cultural performances for tourists.

Banjar meetings normally take place in the wantilan. Every member is expected to attend the routine banjar meetings, called *sangkep*. The banjar members are also strongly expected to participate in all banjar activities. A member who seldom attends meetings or fails to take part in banjar activities will be subject to fines assessed in the form of goods, and will also suffer the social sanction of ostracism.

But banjar members rarely suffer these penalties, because every member recognizes the benefit of participation in the banjar, for both himself and his family. They are therefore happy to participate actively and voluntarily in all banjar activities.

The banjar members are especially happy when they are conducting traditional religious ceremonies; this is evident from the proud, smiling faces and warm, lively atmosphere we see at these times.

The banjar also promulgates the community's traditional rules in the economic, social, religious and agricultural spheres. These rules are known as *awig-awig*. The awig-awig cover many matters, such as building houses, cleaning roads, conducting ceremonies, and so forth; all these activities are done collectively through mutual self-help (*gotong royong*) by all banjar members.

Before the Dutch colonial era, the awig-awig were a purely oral tradition and never written down. After the arrival of the colonialists, who brought with them a written legal system, the awig-awig were also eventually written down, in both the Balinese and the Latin alphabets. This is to make it easier for all banjar members to understand the awig-awig and to reduce the risk of multiple interpretations.

From this, we can see the strong level of trust among banjar members in the past. Based solely on oral consensus, all aspects of community life were organized well and proceeded smoothly. And these same noble spiritual values have been passed down to Bali's communities of today.

Representatives of the banjar are often invited to discuss certain issues at the village or subdistrict level. Conversely, banjar representatives may also be asked to convey to the banjar policies that have been decided at the village/subdistrict or higher levels.

Decisions in the banjar meetings are generally made through deliberation to achieve consensus. This decision-making process in the banjar is often more effective than the decision-making processes used in more formal institutions. Even when the topic under discussion is a serious one, banjar meetings are usually conducted in a friendly, jovial atmosphere, enabling any problems to be more easily resolved.

This form of indigenous democracy has existed for centuries in Balinese society. The banjar is an intrinsic element in the character of Balinese society. The banjar shows that Bali's society has been able to build a sense of community primarily because everyone shares common values. These shared spiritual values that have survived for hundreds of years have enabled the people of Bali to maintain their culture despite the constant influx of influences from outside.

Figure 5.4 Bale Banjar

These strong spiritual values and the intense social solidarity are clearly manifested in the many traditional religious ceremonies that are constantly being held. Two major ceremonies held in Ubud—the great Pelebon in mid 2008, and the Odalan at Pura Gunung Lebah in early 2009—illustrate this.

Pelebon (Ngaben): A Celebration of Life[6]

The *Pelebon* cremation ceremony, also called *Ngaben*, is probably the Hindu-Balinese ritual best known to the outside world. Some major Pelebon have attracted hundreds of thousands of visitors and been reported extensively in the mass media.

A major Pelebon was held in 1979 for three important persons from Ubud who had recently died: the King of Ubud, Tjokorda Gde

Agung Sukawati, and two prominent artists, I Gusti Nyoman Lempad and Rudolf Bonnet. Though the Pelebon rituals should be restricted to members of Hindu-Bali society, certain expatriates deemed to have made great contributions to the development of culture in Ubud, such as Bonnet and Antonio Blanco, have also been honored with Pelebon.

Such massive Pelebon ceremonies are very rarely held. After 1979, it was not until 2008 that another great Pelebon was performed. This Pelebon, which had its climax on 15 July 2008, was attended by tens of thousands of people—some even say 300,000—from the community of Ubud itself, visitors from elsewhere in and outside Bali, and many foreign tourists.

This was a Pelebon on a truly massive scale, because it was the farewell ceremony for Tjokorda Gde Agung Suyasa, who had served as *Penggelisir* of Puri Ubud for three decades. As the head of the Ubud royal family, he was the most highly respected local figure in Ubud following the death of the last King of Ubud, Tjokorda Gde Agung Sukawati.

Tjokorda Gde Agung Suyasa was born on 14 July 1941, the third child of Tjokorda Gde Ngurah and Tjokorda Istri Muter. Tjokorda Gde Agung Suyasa was the older brother of Tjok Ibah (Tjokorda Raka Kerthyasa), and Tjokorda Istri Muter was the twin sister of Tjokorda Gde Agung Sukawati, so Tjokorda Gde Agung Suyasa was a first cousin of Tjok Putra, Tjok Ace, and Tjok 'De.

Apart from Tjokorda Gde Agung Suyasa, the two other prominent persons whose remains were cremated in this Pelebon were Tjokorda Gde Raka, a retired high-ranking police officer from Denpasar, and Gung Niang Desak Raka, another member of the Ubud royal family. The remains of 68 other people from four banjar were also cremated in this massive Pelebon ceremony.

Tjokorda Gde Agung Suyasa passed away on 28 March 2008; the other two main "participants" had passed on well before this Pelebon was conducted. Tjokorda Gde Raka died a week before Tjokorda Gde Agung Suyasa, while Gung Niang Desak Raka died on 23 December 2007.

In Hindu-Balinese society, a Pelebon is not held immediately after someone dies; it must be performed on a propitious day according to the Saka calendar. A reasonable amount of time is also needed for the community to properly prepare everything needed for the ceremony. The Pelebon ceremony actually comprises quite a lengthy process. The ritual performed on 15 July 2008 was the culmination of this process: the cremation itself.

The Balinese calendar is always used to determine the best time to perform any given ceremony; the date is chosen by a *pedanda* (Balinese priest). This is one reason why the remains cannot be cremated straight away. While awaiting the final cremation ceremony, the remains are often kept in the family home, where offerings are made to them every day. Alternatively, the remains may be buried and then disinterred when the Pelebon is ready to be held.

The elaborate preparations for this major Pelebon began well in advance. People from Ubud of all ages and social strata worked together to build the *bade* (a nine-level cremation tower symbolizing the levels of life), create a Lembu or giant ox statue as the sarcophagus (the container for the remains during the cremation), and prepare all the other trappings needed for the various ceremonies. They did all this with very simple tools such as knives and machetes, and using locally available natural materials such as bamboo, wood, coconut fronds, rattan, black palm fibers (*ijuk*), and so on.

All the preparations, which were carried out either inside or near Puri Ubud, were supervised directly by the royal family, and were open to anyone who wanted to pitch in or simply to watch. Quite a few foreign tourists witnessed the preparations for this great Pelebon.

Once everything was ready, on the appointed day, the Pelebon rituals began. First, the community of Ubud performed prayers in the presence of all the remains to be cremated, led by pedanda in the courtyard of Puri Ubud. Then, around noon, the coffin containing the remains of Tjokorda Gde Agung Suyasa was placed in the bade, which was a stunning 28.5 meters high and weighed 11 tons—the tallest bade ever made in the history of Ubud. The bade was design and constructed by

Tjok 'De. The bade was then carried by thousands of Ubud residents in purple uniforms to Pura Dalem Puri Peliatan, around one kilometer east of Puri Ubud.

The atmosphere became quite tense when the coffin was being placed on the bade. Several people climbed tall bamboo ladders and slowly transferred the coffin to the highest level of the bade. You can imagine how suspenseful this was, since the bade was so tall and no special equipment was being used.

Also borne in this procession was the Lembu sarcophagus, a huge statue in the form of a black ox with its horns and tail decorated in gold. There was also a statue of a dragon with a long tail, called *Naga Banda,* which is only used in pelebon for members of the Ubud royal family and therefore rarely seen.

The procession was led by the Ubud royal family, who were being carried on the bade. They directed the bearers and occasionally sprinkled water on them to relieve their fatigue. During this procession to the cremation venue, long poles were repeatedly used to lift electricity and telephone wires so the bade could pass below. The bade was then paraded around in various directions three times; this is done to disorient the spirit of the person whose remains are about to be cremated, so that it does not find its way back home and disturb the family.

The procession took several hours, so it was nearly sunset when it arrived at the cremation venue. Once the procession had reached the venue, the remains were transferred into the ox statue and burnt. All the other ritual paraphernalia, including the bade and the Naga Banda, were burnt as well. Once the cremation process was complete, the ashes would be later thrown into the sea at Sanur beach, as a symbol of their final return to nature.

The purpose of the Pelebon is to restore the physical remains of the person who has passed away to their original constituent elements, and to release the person's soul from its earthly bonds.

In Hindu-Balinese belief, the human soul resides within the body, which is a small "vessel" (microcosm). When a person dies, his soul (in Balinese called *atma*) remains present near the body. The five elements that form the body—fire, air, water, earth, and ether—must be returned to the natural universe, the greater "vessel" (macrocosm), and the person's soul will thereby be released to find its way to God. This, in brief, is the significance of the Pelebon ceremony.

So though it is in fact a funeral ritual, it is conducted in a joyous atmosphere—no sad faces here. Raucous gamelan music accompanies the procession. Tjok Ibah, a spokesman for the royal family, put it this way: "The Pelebon is not a mourning ritual; rather, we see it as a way to console the spirits of those who have passed away and ensure that they are not disturbed by the tears and wailing of those left behind." For this reason, the theme of the great Pelebon held in 2008 was "Celebration of Life".

This particular Pelebon was also professionally packaged as an event to attract tourists. The Indonesian Department of Culture and Tourism included it as part of its Visit Indonesia 2008 program. Indonesia's leading public relations firm, IndoPacific Edelman, operated the Media Center. Information on this ceremony can also be accessed on the Internet through several blogs, including http://pelebon2008.blogspot.com.

The atmosphere surrounding this Pelebon was harmonious, convivial, and full of voluntary spirit. The community of Ubud were excellent hosts. Local women offered free snacks, tea and coffee to visitors. The *pecalang* (traditional security guards) maintained order in the dense crowds; it was difficult to move at all, let alone walk. Some people climbed onto the roofs of buildings to be able to witness the ceremony.

So we can see that this Pelebon was far more than simply a religious ceremony to dispose of human remains. Such ceremonies also stimulate the local economy by actively involving all the banjar in Ubud. The people of Ubud all worked together to make the ceremony a success, with no thought of material compensation. And the local people cooperated well with the visitors, so the entire process went quite smoothly.

All the items used in the rituals—the bade, the Lembu and Naga Banda statues, the firewood, the offerings—were made entirely from local, natural materials. So when all these objects were burned, they were reduced to ashes and easily reunited with nature.

This was a genuine manifestation of Tri Hita Karana, with harmonious relations between humankind and God, among humans, and between humans and the natural universe.

This Pelebon also demonstrated how modern technology, such as the Internet, can be used to disseminate information on the living culture of Ubud. In this way, people around the world were able to learn more about Ubud without actually visiting.

Figure 5.5 The Lembu sarcophagus (courtesy of Puri Ubud)

Figure 5.6 The Naga Banda statue (courtesy of Puri Ubud)

Figure 5.7 The cremation (courtesy of Puri Ubud)

Odalan: The Temple Anniversary[7]

Another major traditional religious event is the Odalan ceremony held at large temples. This ceremony is held to celebrate the anniversary of a temple, once every 210 days (one year in the Balinese Saka calendar). The Odalan rituals are performed by the people living near the pura and go on for several days. These rituals include purification of the temple's sacred *barong*, presentation of offerings, and prayers, accompanied by gamelan music and dances to honor the gods.

An Odalan was held from 7 to 10 January 2009 at Pura Gunung Lebah. Because this is such a historically important pura, the Odalan was a large one. Preparations began three months beforehand, and involved several villages and banjar in the Ubud area, under the direct supervision of the Ubud royal family.

Just like for any other birthday party, the atmosphere at the Odalan for Pura Gunung Lebah was joyous. Seen from a distance, the pura was blanketed in golden yellow from all the ritual paraphernalia.

All along the road to the pura and within the pura itself were *penjor* (tall decorated bamboo poles posted in front of buildings on special occasions, symbolizing Gunung Agung). Apart from the penjor, other decorations inside the pura included red, yellow and white pennants (*umbul-umbul*) adorned with paintings of green dragons; *lamak* (long banners decorated with certain motifs, made from palm leaves); decorated spears; and replicas of the pura containing offerings to welcome the gods. The statue of Rsi Markandya was also dressed in a pale yellow and white wraparound cloth (*kain*) like those worn by priests.

All the structures of Pura Gunung Lebah, including the *bale kulkul*, were covered with ornamental cloth or paper in golden yellow hues. Dozens of banten filled every corner of the pura.

All these decorations and offerings were prepared collectively by the people of Ubud. For an entire week before the ceremony, around 400 people were working in turns every day from nine in the morning until late at night. They came from various banjar and other community organizations in Ubud, including hotel employees, market traders, and so on. Children as well as adults took part in the preparations for the Odalan.

Men performed the heavy work, such as erecting tents made of wood and bamboo, setting up the lighting, and affixing the decorations, while the women mostly prepared banten and refreshments.

During these preparations, it was obvious that everyone already knew what needed to be done. No one had to be told or instructed, since they had all been doing this for many years. Children took part by watching and helping with the lighter work, thereby becoming familiar with these routine preparations. And this is how culture and customs are passed down from generation to generation.

The Odalan ceremony itself began in the early evening with the arrival of delegations from various banjar in Ubud. This was a lively event in itself, as each group walked there from its banjar. At the front of each procession were children carrying umbul-umbul, followed in turn by rows of married men carrying heirloom banners (*panji*) and umbrellas, rows of married women carrying banten on their heads, rows of young men carrying temple replicas and the sacred barong, and finally a gamelan marching band.

The participants in the Odalan ceremony were neatly dressed. The women wore traditional Balinese blouses (*kebaya*), in different uniform colors for each banjar or group. Most of the men were dressed identically, with white headcloths (*udeng*), white shirts, and sarongs, either brown batik or black-and-white checked.

All the ritual accessories were carried into the temple. The musicians played the gamelan instruments they carried, accompanied now and then by dances. The gamelan players and dancers included children as well as adults. Each banjar took its turn to give its own special performance.

At the Odalan ceremony, we can see the sacred *barong*[8] from the various temples in and around Ubud. Though they look quite similar, these sacred barong are not the same ones we see in dance performances. These sacred barong cannot be made by just anyone; only people with a high level of spirituality can be entrusted with this task, and the process involves a series of special rituals. And the sacred barong are displayed only at certain special times.

Once they arrived at the pura, the sacred barong took turns being purified with holy water on a hill behind the temple. The atmosphere surrounding this purification ceremony was quite mystical, as it was performed in an isolated location and at night. The lighting was minimal—just a few flashlights and portable electric lights carried by the barong bearers. The barong bearers crowded the footpath on the hill, awaiting their barong's turn.

After they were ritually cleansed, the barong were brought back into the temple and hung at specified locations. Certain parts—the heads and backs of the barong—were bound with ropes to the pillars of the pura buildings, and wooden blocks were used to support the heavier, lower parts of the barong.

Apart from the bearers of the sacred barong, the other participants in the Odalan ceremony, who filled all corners of Pura Gunung Lebah, were all engaged in various activities. Many were deeply absorbed in prayers led by the pedanda; others were getting ready for their performances, eating together, or simply chatting.

A number of foreign tourists also watched the ceremony, mingled with the local people, and avidly photographed or videoed the proceedings. For these foreign tourists, personally witnessing a traditional religious ceremony like this Odalan is an unforgettable experience.

Observing and being directly involved in such a cultural event is indeed a rare treat. We may have watched many performances of Balinese music and dance, but only as part of a paying audience, and only seeing the final result on a fairly small stage. At the Odalan, on the other hand, we can be involved in the entire process from the beginning and witness an authentic cultural event that is not limited by a stage.

This makes it a truly memorable inner experience. Where else could we witness such an authentic cultural event? Where else would we see the purification ritual of so many sacred barong?

The Odalan rituals take place in a reverent yet joyous atmosphere. They are open to all; anyone can take part in the ceremonies, as long as they abide by local customs. For example, they must dress properly and behave respectfully during the rituals. Tourists are even welcome to eat with the local people and taste the authentic traditional dishes prepared for this special event.

The main event of the Odalan ceremony is called *Puncak Karya*. This ritual, which takes place on the first day, is aimed at harmonizing the temple and the surrounding villages. An equally exciting event takes place on the fifth or last day: the highly magical Calon Arang performance.

The atmosphere outside Pura Gunung Lebah was also quite lively. In the courtyard of Kerta Yoga Junior High School across from the temple, there was a small bazaar where vendors were hawking *mie bakso* (noodle and meatball soup), instant noodles, *sate lilit* (Balinese-style spiced meat twisted onto skewers and grilled), soft drinks, fried snacks, candy and toys.

The excitement from the event could be seen, heard and even felt from Jalan Raya Sanggingan. Despite the crowds, everything remained safe and orderly; the pecalang brought in from the various banjar had very little trouble keeping matters under control.

The Odalan ceremony is yet another proof that the values of social solidarity and mutual self-help remain strong in the community of Ubud. Everyone participates to the best of their ability. It is this kind of collective community work that shapes the unique character of Ubud.

And again, we note that traditional religious ceremonies such as the Odalan are more than simply a form of worship; they are also social events where all elements of the community come together in celebration, and of course they stimulate the local economy as well.

Figure 5.8 Odalan ceremony preparation at Pura Gunung Lebah

Figure 5.9 Odalan ceremony at Pura Gunung Lebah

Figure 5.10 The sacred Barong

Figure 5.11 The prayers

Figure 5.12 Tourists watching the Odalan ceremony

The spirituality inherent in these cultural and social activities is, as we put it, the element that creates the DNA of Ubud. Consequently, despite the constant physical changes in the temporal world, Ubud's character will be preserved and Ubud will always retain its strong sense of *taksu*.

The elements forming this "Ubud DNA" can be seen in many aspects, both concrete and abstract. Earlier we described the various religious and cultural ceremonies and the banjar system practiced by the community of Ubud. There are a number of other, seemingly trivial things that also contribute to shaping the character of Ubud.

For instance, there's a tendency not to use plastic. We all know that plastic will only decompose after many decades. For this reason, the use of plastic is strictly limited, to prevent damage to the environment.

The placing of flowers on statues is another example. A statue with flowers on it exerts a stronger attraction; it seems to emanate love; flowers on a statue give it a very different aura.

Outside influences have also played an important role in shaping Ubud's character. The carving designs in the temple buildings have Javanese elements, and the gamelan instruments originally came from Java. Likewise, the Balinese barong strongly resembles the Chinese *barongsay*. But all of these have undergone adaptations and become typically Balinese.

This cultural assimilation is a bit surprising, since Ubud is situated in the interior of Bali, far from the coastal areas, which are normally more receptive to outside influences. Certainly, the inclusiveness and openness of Ubud's society results in part from the presence of tourists for so many decades.

This spirit of maintaining the noble values of the past, while remaining open to those new values that are recognized as good, is an attitude inherent in all residents of Ubud. It is this spirit that has given Ubud its unique character and its strong taksu.

Everything in Ubud has this taksu. And for this reason, it's difficult to identify any one thing that could be considered the "icon" of Ubud. Singapore has Orchard Road, Kuala Lumpur has the Petronas Twin

Towers, Yogyakarta has Candi Borobudur, and Jakarta has the National Monument (Monas)—so what is the icon of Ubud?

It's a hard question to answer; maybe impossible. Tjok Putra says that to display an icon of Ubud, all you need to do is take a photograph of a leaf falling off a tree in Ubud, or of Ubud's clear blue sky. These things can be taken as representative of Ubud, because the leaf and the sky embody Ubud's strong spiritual aura.

It is this aura that differentiates Ubud from other places with equally attractive scenery—Switzerland, for example. The natural panorama, and indeed all the attractive visible aspects of Ubud, is merely the outward form of Ubud's taksu. The essence, the content, is the feeling that emerges within ourselves.

Taksu is a difficult concept to express in words; it can only be felt in the heart. It is this feeling that enables us to fall in love with Ubud; it's what explains why many people cry when they have to leave Ubud, as if they were parting from a loved one.

(Endnotes)

1   Nyepi is the celebration of the New Year in the Hindu-Bali Saka calendar. During Nyepi, the Hindu-Balinese abstain from four things, called *Catur Brata: amati geni* (light no fires or lamps), *amati lelungan* (do not go out of the house), *amati lelanguan* (no entertainment), and *amati karya* (no work).

2   *Canang* are offerings for daily or small rituals, while *banten* are offerings for major ceremonies; banten are thus more complete than canang. A canang consists of a small square box of woven *janur* (young coconut leaves), usually containing a pinch of cooked rice, a bit of fried grated coconut placed on a banana leaf, several types of flowers, leaves, biscuits, and incense sticks. Banten are usually placed in larger containers—bamboo baskets or round aluminum trays—and contain fruit, cakes, eggs, rice, canang, and sometimes roast chickens.

3   A *meru* is a tower with an odd number of levels—anywhere from one to eleven. The Hindu-Balinese believe that odd numbers indicate balance, both in the natural world and in human life. The meru symbolize the mountains that are believed to support the natural universe.

4   The *bale kulkul* is a small building that contains the *kulkul*, an alarm consisting of a length of bamboo or wooden tubing that is struck with a stick, usually to produce warning signals. The kulkul in the temple is only sounded when there is a ceremony or other community event, to summon everyone to the temple. Each activity has its own special signal. Because of its function, the bale kulkul is always in some high spot, either in a separate building or even in a tree.

5   This description of Pura Gunung Lebah is based on visits to the temple itself and an interview with Tjok Putra and Tjok 'De, as well as other sources.

6   This description of the Pelebon is based on our attendance at the Great Pelebon of 15 July 2008, interviews with Tjok 'De, and other sources.

7   This description of the Odalan is based on our attendance at the Odalan on 7-10 January 2009 and the guidebook for the ceremony.

8   The *barong* is a mystical character with a physical form resembling a wild animal that is a symbol of goodness and a protector of holy places. The barong's enemy is a character named Rangda. The conflict between the Barong and Rangda is one of the themes most often portrayed in Balinese cultural performances.

Chapter 6

The Food Paradise

"It is not just the culture that has kindled my love for Bali.
It is also the food."
Janet DeNeefe

One of the major attractions of Ubud is its culinary tourism. In Ubud we can enjoy a wide variety of cuisines—not just traditional Balinese dishes and food from elsewhere in Indonesia, but also taste treats from all over the world. The venues for these feasts vary as well—everything from *warung* (simple, traditional food stalls) to fine dining restaurants like those in any world metropolis. With this diversity, it's no wonder that one nickname for Ubud is "the food paradise".

Apart from the cuisine itself, equally interesting is the process to produce it. For the Hindu-Balinese, cooking is not merely a way to meet our physical needs but also part of the culture and, indeed, a form of art. For this reason, food preparation is performed very precisely and can take quite a long time.

The Hindu-Balinese also have a tradition of cooking using only fresh ingredients available at the time; they never use preserved foodstuffs. And the food that is cooked is almost always eaten up the same day; "leftovers" is an alien concept.

Furthermore, for the Hindu-Balinese, cooking is also a form of devotion to Almighty God. Most of the traditional Balinese dishes we know today, such as grilled chicken or roast suckling pig, were formerly prepared only for traditional religious ceremonies. These dishes only began to be served in restaurants after tourism became a major industry.

Restaurants began to develop in Bali in the 1970s. Though foreigners have been visiting since the 1930s, there weren't many restaurants because many of the early visitors were artists who stayed in local people's homes, where they also took most of their meals. It was only in the 1970s, when a greater variety of tourists started coming and the tourism sector in Bali began to expand, that restaurants started appearing one by one.

Given this background, it's understandable that Ubud continues to strongly uphold its Hindu-Balinese values and culture; there are no fast-food restaurants or international outlets such as McDonald's or Starbucks. The food processing in fast-food restaurants tends to be standardized, using mechanical equipment, without the human touch that characterizes works of art.

Furthermore, the presence of fast-food restaurants, using materials from outside Ubud, would also conflict with the prevailing values of social solidarity. The people of Ubud would gain little benefit from fast-food restaurants; such places could even create social problems.

But this does not mean that the people of Ubud shut themselves off to food from outside Bali. The people of Ubud recognize that not all newcomers and tourists in Ubud would necessarily find traditional Balinese cuisine to their liking. And so we also find in Ubud food from other regions of Indonesia—Padang restaurants, or goat saté from Madura. There are also many restaurants in Ubud serving international food from Asia and Europe.

These restaurants eventually became meeting places where all kinds of people come together and interact, and not simply places to fill one's stomach. Restaurants are the venues for discussions on many topics. If the natives of Ubud have the *banjar* as their meeting places, the tourists and expatriates gather in restaurants.

Many restaurants are now equipped with Internet hot spot facilities, so we can enjoy great food, engage in lively discussions, and surf the net in comfort. Quite a few restaurants also offer cooking classes, so we can learn how to prepare these dishes ourselves.

Thus, food and restaurants have become an inseparable part of the culture that has developed in Ubud. Once again, the dishes that we enjoy not only serve to meet our physical needs, but are also works of art to appreciate. And restaurants are not places simply for eating, but also for human interaction.

A number of restaurants in Ubud have become legends among food lovers, both for their food and for other reasons. Below are the stories of a few of these restaurants, some established by native Ubudians and some by expatriates.

Murni's Warung[1]

Murni's Warung was probably the first restaurant in Ubud to become popular among tourists, especially foreigners. It's located on Jalan Raya Sanggingan, directly opposite the old iron bridge from the Dutch colonial days known simply as The Bridge.

The founder and owner of this restaurant is Ni Wayan Murni; this is why it's called Murni's Warung. The restaurant has a long history. Ibu Murni started out as a salt trader in the 1950s when she was not yet ten. She had to carry large baskets of salt from her home in the northern part of Ubud to Desa Penestanan, around two kilometers away.

Also when she was very young, her parents separated. Little Murni went to live with her aunt in Denpasar. There she had to get up at two in the morning and sell food until five, before going off to school.

Some time later, young Murni returned to Ubud and lived with her mother. They had a small shop in Pasar Ubud where they sold products such as beer, soft drinks, and batik to foreign tourists. At the time, theirs was the only stall in the market that sold beer and soft drinks, so drinks were often purchased from their stall to entertain guests at Puri Ubud. And President Soekarno, who often visited Ubud, once bought some of their batik.

In the early 1970s, Murni opened her own shop on a small plot of land on Jalan Raya Sanggingan—the venue of the present restaurant—which she rented from a man named Pak Munut. The shop sold sarongs, carvings and paintings. Ibu Murni was no cook, so it didn't occur to her to open a food stall. And there was very little furniture, just one bamboo table and two chairs.

There was a customer from the United States, one Patrick Moore Scanland, who often asked Ibu Murni to make him sandwiches and beer at the warung. Eventually, many other guests wanted the same, and that was the start of Murni's Warung.

In 1974, Ibu Murni married Patrick. One year later, they bought the land and opened the restaurant, Murni's Warung. At the same time, they opened an antique shop with a collection of art works from all parts of Asia.

Murni's Warung had, and has, a very loyal clientele. The customers helped promote Murni's Warung and taught Ibu Murni how to cook Western food. This is how Murni's Warung became known as the first restaurant in Ubud to offer Western food to tourists.

The architectural design of Murni's Warung is in traditional Balinese style, with an open air concept. The building has four stories, going downward from street level, as it is built on the banks of the Oos River. There are paintings and statues throughout the restaurant; one of the most interesting portrays the scene around Murni's Warung in the 1970s.

On one story, there is a room for private special events, called The Lounge. Inside The Lounge, there's a large statue of Ganesha. On the lowest level, we can enjoy our food while watching the Oos flowing past.

The favorite dishes here are Nasi Campur Bali (rice with various side dishes), Nasi Goreng (fried rice), and typical Indonesian drinks such as *cendol* and sweet iced tea. As well as traditional dishes, Murni's Warung offers many other choices.

In addition to the food, as mentioned earlier, Murni's Warung has an antique store that sells a variety of souvenirs and antiques from throughout Indonesia: textiles, statues, traditional heirlooms, paintings and so on. Ibu Murni herself often travels abroad and collects antiques from the countries she visits to display and sell in the shop.

The present building of Murni's Warung is very different from the original structure built in 1974. The present building is the result of a major renovation in 1992, but the traditional Balinese architecture remains the same.

Figure 6.1 Murni's Warung

Warung Babi Guling Ibu Oka[2]

Warung Babi Guling Ibu Oka is on Jalan Suweta, right next to Puri Ubud. Because of this strategic location, and of course the food, this warung is constantly busy from opening time at midday until it closes in the late afternoon. Many people are willing to wait quite a while to enjoy the specialty, *babi guling*—roast suckling pig—at this fairly small warung.

This babi guling business was started by Anak Agung Biang Tu and carried on by her daughter-in-law, Anak Agung Oka Sinar. Ibu Oka is now over 60; Ibu Biang Tu passed away in 1973.

Ibu Biang Tu started selling roast suckling pig around the Pasar Ubud area in the 1950s. She sold babi guling only when traditional religious ceremonies were taking place. In those days, there was no fixed venue; she sold her product by carrying it around on her head. This remained the case until Ibu Biang Tu passed away. Only later, in the late 1980s, did Ibu Oka open the present warung selling babi guling.

The roast suckling pig is cooked in a house, also on Jalan Suweta, around 50 meters from the food stall: Ibu Oka's family home. Aside from being the place where the pigs are slaughtered and cooked, the house is also sometimes the temporary location of Warung Babi Guling Ibu Oka when it is closed because of other activities near the warung.

Each day, up to five pigs, purchased from local livestock raisers, are slaughtered. The pigs are slaughtered at around three in the morning, seasoned with special spices, and then roasted on spits over coffee wood fires. The skin is coated with a mixture of coconut oil and turmeric, giving it a golden yellow color. The roasting process takes around five hours, so the meat is tender and thoroughly imbued with the spices. The babi guling is then taken to the warung, so it's always fresh.

If you want, you can watch the process, and even help to turn the spits. Obviously, you have to ask permission beforehand and get up very early to watch the entire process from the start. But where else could you enjoy such a unique experience?

Warung Babi Guling Ibu Oka is very popular with foreign tourists. The warung was in the "Global Glutton Suckling Pig" list in *Esquire* magazine's October 2007 edition, along with restaurants from France, England, Mexico, Spain, and the U.S. It has also been featured in the program "No Reservations" broadcast on the *Discovery Travel & Living* TV channel, hosted by Anthony Bourdain. The Miele Restaurant Guide, Asia's leading restaurant guide, awarded Warung Babi Guling Ibu Oka the title "One of Asia's Finest Restaurants 2008/2009".

The warung is so popular that many people have offered to open branches in other cities, or just to buy the name. But Ibu Oka and her family aren't interested. Unlike other dishes, this babi guling has to be prepared in exactly the right way; not just anyone knows how to do it. So there are no franchises in other cities; Warung Babi Guling Ibu Oka is only found in Ubud.

To accommodate the huge number of customers, in late 2008 a branch of the warung was opened in Teges, near Museum Rudana. This second warung is bigger, with two stories, and can accommodate around 300 people. Since the second warung opened, the queues at the original warung have subsided somewhat, so customers can now enjoy their meals in greater comfort.

Figure 6.2 Warung Babi Guling Ibu Oka

Nasi Ayam Kedewatan Ibu Mangku[3]

Warung Nasi Ayam Kedewatan Ibu Mangku is located right beside the road on Jalan Raya Kedewatan. At first glance, it looks small, but it has a large rear courtyard. And though it's quite basic, this warung has long been a favorite with such notables as Megawati Soekarnoputri and Guruh Soekarnoputra.

The warung was established by Ibu Mangku, who is now 67. It has a long history. Speaking in a very refined manner, Ibu Mangku told us that when she was younger, she didn't sell food. From childhood to her adolescence in the 1950s, she gathered plants from the mountains to sell in Pasar Ubud.

In 1963, around the time Gunung Agung erupted, she got married and became pregnant with her first child. Ibu Mangku started selling coffee, since her physical condition no longer allowed her to carry heavy loads.

In 1965, she opened her stall selling chicken and rice, located on Jalan Raya Kedewatan a bit south of the present location. It was a very simple warung, with only one table. In 1980, Ibu Mangku opened a warung at her husband's home, and this is the one we see today.

Warung Nasi Ayam Kedewatan Ibu Mangku is now managed by Ibu Mangku's younger sister, Sang Ayu Rani. Since she's getting on in years, Ibu Mangku only looks in at her warung now and then. She spends much of her time preparing traditional religious ceremonies, for example making *banten,* so the management of the warung is entirely in her sister's hands. But Sang Ayu Rani has been helping out with the cooking and running the warung since she was very young, so she's totally familiar with the operation.

As the name suggests, there is only one item on the menu here: *Nasi Ayam*—chicken and rice, consisting of a plate of white rice served with *ayam betutu,* shredded chicken, liver and gizzard, *saté lilit,* half a boiled egg, and *urap* (spicy vegetables with grated coconut). We can enjoy our nasi ayam sitting at a table or *lesehan* style on a mat in the front room, or in one of the pavilions in the rear courtyard.

The warung, which is only open from midday till late afternoon, now has two branches, one in Renon, Denpasar and the other in Seminyak. Both branches have more space than the original warung in Desa Kedewatan.

Apart from Nasi Ayam Kedewatan Ibu Mangku, there's another well-known chicken and rice stall called Nasi Ayam Kedewatan Mardika, also on Jalan Raya Kedewatan, just 20 meters north of Ibu Mangku's. Warung Mardika was started by Ibu Sang Putu Mardika in 1972. The menu is essentially the same, but Ibu Mardika's nasi ayam is a bit spicier.

Figure 6.3 Warung Nasi Ayam Kedewatan Ibu Mangku

Café Wayan[4]

Don't let the name "Café" mislead you; this is actually a restaurant. Café Wayan, on Jalan Monkey Forest, is one of the oldest and best known restaurants in Ubud.

Café Wayan started as a simple warung, first opened by Ibu Wayan Kelepon back in 1977. She sold black sticky rice porridge (*bubur ketan hitam*) and coffee to farmers in the Jalan Monkey Forest area, which was then still mostly farmland.

Gradually, as the tourism business developed in Ubud, tourists also began to visit the warung. They bought coffee and snacks, and also peanuts to feed to the monkeys in the Monkey Forest.

Since she had always enjoyed cooking, Ibu Wayan started serving traditional Balinese food. She also started learning Western recipes from her customers. Ibu Wayan's skill in preparing international dishes grew tremendously when she began traveling abroad. She studied Western cuisine with Chef Joe Schultz from India Joe's restaurant in Santa Cruz, California, and also studied Thai cooking in Bangkok.

In 1986, Ibu Wayan opened Café Wayan. What was at first a very basic warung has now become a full-sized restaurant covering half a hectare and seating 150. The restaurant is in traditional Balinese style, with an outdoor concept. Guests can enjoy their meals either seated conventionally at a table or sitting on mats (*lesehan* style) in one of the many *bale* (Balinese gazebos) in the restaurant's garden. The buildings and the garden were designed by Pak Ketut, Ibu Wayan's husband.

In addition to traditional Balinese dishes, including Nasi Campur Bali, Café Wayan is also famous for its cocktails, chocolate cakes, and croissants. They also offer cooking classes, taught by Ibu Wayan herself and her daughter, Wayan Metri. Participants in the cooking classes can learn how to prepare traditional Balinese dishes in two-hour sessions, between 10 AM and 4 PM.

Café Wayan is now being managed by Ibu Wayan's son-in-law, Mangku Pardita. To keep up with the tremendous demand from tourists, Café Wayan has also opened a sister restaurant, Laka Leke, in Desa Nyuhkuning, behind the Monkey Forest.

Figure 6.4 Café Wayan

Bebek Bengil[5]

Perhaps the favorite restaurant among domestic tourists is Restoran Bebek Bengil (Dirty Duck Diner). This restaurant as strategically located on Jalan Hanoman, near the three-way intersection leading to the Monkey Forest. It's also very comfortable. The combination of tasty food, strategic location, and comfortable venue means that this restaurant is always packed.

The road out front is always full of parked cars, especially during holidays. It's so popular that they have imposed a waiting list system. If the restaurant is full, visitors are asked to give their names and wait in the lobby until they are called, when someone else has finished eating. Though this is a bit of a bother, people are willing to wait. Some leave their names and then go sightseeing and come back an hour or two later.

The restaurant's name is quite unusual. Here's the story: In 1990, when construction of the restaurant was nearly finished, the proprietors, a couple named Anak Agung Gde Raka and Anak Agung Raka Sueni, still hadn't thought of a suitable name. They wanted a name that was typically Balinese but also memorable when translated into English.

One morning in the rainy season, a flock of ducks from the rice paddy across the road swarmed into the restaurant, quacking noisily and leaving muddy footprints all over the place.

And this is where they got the idea to name the restaurant "Bebek Bengil", after the dirty ducks (*bengil* is Balinese for "dirty") that were its first guests.

The restaurant has been very popular ever since it opened. Bebek Bengil became even more famous after a customer from Canada named Tamara promoted it to her friends by word of mouth.

Bebek Bengil covers around one hectare and accommodates up to 350 persons. In the early days, there were only eleven tables, but the place was gradually expanded in 1998 and again in 2000.

The design concept here is open space, with dozens of small pavilions and several lily ponds in a shady garden. Behind the restaurant are green rice fields. The atmosphere in the evening is exotic and romantic, with minimal lighting.

The main item on the menu is, of course, fried duck. The restaurant's full name is "Bebek Bengil Original Sejak 1990" (Original Dirty Duck - Since 1990). This dish was created by a cook named Wayan Sandi, who still works there.

This signature dish consists of a plate of hot white rice, half a fairly large fried duck, *urap*, cucumber, and Balinese *sambal matah*, a hot sauce with thin slices of red shallots and *terasi* (fermented shrimp paste). The duck meat it soft and flavorful; even the bones are crunchy and edible. Just imagine how tasty this is…

Many famous people, from Indonesia and abroad, have sampled the food at Bebek Bengil. Indonesian presidents such as Susilo Bambang Yudhoyono and Megawati Soekarnoputri have eaten here, as have Hong Kong actor Chow Yun-Fat and legendary musicians Mick Jagger and Sting.

Bebek Bengil is now operated by Anak Agung Raka Sueni alone, since her husband, Anak Agung Gde Raka, passed away. Bebek Bengil also has an outlet in Jakarta, on Jalan Haji Agus Salim in Menteng, which opened in February 2009. But all the spices, ingredients, and even the cooks come from the original restaurant in Ubud, so the taste is exactly the same. When we miss being in Ubud, a visit to Bebek Bengil in Jakarta helps soothe our longings and reinforces our emotional bond with Ubud.

Figure 6.5 Bebek Bengil

Indus and Casa Luna[6]

Indus and Casa Luna are two restaurants that are very popular with international tourists. Both were established and are managed by a couple, Ketut Suardana and Janet DeNeefe. Indus Restaurant is located on Jalan Raya Sanggingan, while Casa Luna is on Jalan Raya Ubud, opposite Museum Puri Lukisan.

Janet is an expatriate from Melbourne, Australia, who came to Bali in 1974. Apart from running the restaurants, Janet is also known as a writer. She has written a book, *Fragrant Rice* (published in 2003), and writes a regular column for the Garuda Indonesia in-flight magazine. Janet is also the founder of one of the international events regularly held in Ubud, the Ubud Writers & Readers Festival.

Both restaurants have unusual names. Indus is the name of one of the world's great rivers, which flows from Tibet through India and Pakistan and empties into the Arabian Sea. This river was home to one of the world's earliest civilizations. The name of the country India is derived from the word "Indus". The name Casa Luna comes from Spanish; *casa* means "house" and *luna* means "moon". The name Casa Luna was inspired by Janet's experiences in Spain.

Indus Restaurant was opened on 2 November 1998, and Casa Luna on 10 July 1992. Janet DeNeefe previously ran another restaurant called Lilies in the mid 1980s, but it closed in 1991.

Indus Restaurant has two stories and can accommodate up to 200 people. Unlike many other restaurants, this one is open all day, from 7.30 AM until 10.30 PM. It also features live jazz and Latin music at certain times.

The view from Indus is spectacular, overlooking the Tjampuhan Hills; when the weather is clear, you can also see majestic Gunung Agung off in the distance. The atmosphere is even more romantic in the evening, when the restaurant is illuminated only by candlelight.

The menu here is quite varied. There's Balinese nasi campur, with *saté lilit*, chicken, tofu, and three veg—long beans, squash, and swamp cabbage (*kangkung*). There's also a wide range of Western dishes and seafood. For drinks, you can choose from sweet iced tea, young coconut, various types of juice, or the famous local wine from Bali, Wine of the Gods.

The atmosphere is cozy, so tourists and expatriates who visit Indus often chat late into the evening. As well as more conventional tables and chairs, Indus also offers seating on mats on the floor (*lesehan*)—a very comfortable way to sit and chat. In addition to the restaurant, Indus also has a small gallery selling paintings and antiques.

Casa Luna, with three stories, is also quite popular with tourists because of its strategic location. In addition to Indonesian food, the menu here features a number of dishes Janet has enjoyed abroad. Casa Luna is also home to the Casa Luna Cooking School, for those who are interested in learning to prepare these tasty dishes.

Figure 6.6 Indus

Figure 6.7 Casa Luna

Mozaic Restaurant[7]

Mozaic Restaurant is situated on Jalan Raya Sanggingan, not far from Indus. This restaurant is operated by Chris Salans, son of a French mother and an American father. Chris was born in Washington, D.C. and moved to Paris at the age of two.

Chris studied at the Cordon Bleu cooking school in Paris, and later cooked at several places in Europe, the U.S., and Singapore, including the French restaurant-bistro Bouchon in California's Napa Valley. He then moved to Bali and served as head chef at Ary's Warung for three years before opening his own restaurant, Mozaic.

With his personal background growing up in France—one of the world's most renowned culinary centers—and his long experience as a chef, Chris's expertise in food preparation and restaurant management is beyond doubt. Mozaic Restaurant is one of the best "fine dining" restaurants in Ubud, and therefore quite popular with both tourists and expatriates.

Mozaic has won great international acclaim, including an award from the Miele Restaurant Guide among "the 5th Asia's Finest Restaurants 2008/2009"; one of the two restaurants in Southeast Asia selected by Traditions et Qualité as a member of *Les Grandes Tables du Monde 2009* (Great Tables of the World 2009); high praise from Condé Nast Traveler magazine; and an extensive wine cellar that earned the "Award of Excellence 2008" from *Wine Spectator* magazine.

Although the restaurant refers to its food as "Modern Balinese Cuisine", the dishes served are not limited to Balinese styles. A variety of dishes, including of course French, are also served here. Chris also runs a cooking school for those who wish to learn the culinary arts.

In an interview with the Bali Advertiser tabloid, Chris Salans said that he wants to make Mozaic "a destination restaurant"—a place that people want to visit, that they will come back to time and again and tell their friends about, not just a place people go to because they happen to be nearby. To be such a destination, Mozaic offers high-quality food, top-rate service, and a comfortable atmosphere.

Naughty Nuri's[8]

Unlike other restaurants in Ubud that serve Western food, Naughty Nuri's Warung looks very basic. This warung on Jalan Raya Sanggingan across from Museum Neka is, as the name implies, a traditional food stall, with wooden chairs and long tables and a green tin roof with the name "Nuri's" painted on it.

But don't be deceived by its outward appearance. This warung is very popular among Western tourists. Many world celebrities have sampled the food here, including Donna Karan, Dolph Lundgren, and Anthony Bourdain.

Naughty Nuri's was started by a couple, Isnuri Suryatmi and Brian Aldinger, in November 1995 with only a two-burner cooker and one icebox. On opening day, they had two bottles of Fanta, two of Coca-Cola, two Sprites, and three large and three small bottles of beer.

At first, they served only Indonesian food. The warung started serving barbecue—now its mainstay—after Brian, who comes from New York, was urged by his friends to cook it for them.

Naughty Nuri's now gets through 500 kilograms of pork ribs per week. Other favorites at this warung include the hamburgers and its signature Martini. *Frommer's* guide says that Naughty Nuri's has "the best barbecue in town".

Jazz Café[9]

The Jazz Café, located on Jalan Tebesaya (also sometimes called Jalan Sukma) is known not so much its food as for the live music and unique interior.

The owner of the Jazz Café is a musician, I Gusti Bagus Agung Wiriawan, who opened it in December 1996. At that time, there were no restaurants in Ubud with live music, so Agung Wiriawan had the idea of starting this café. He's a jazz lover, and he thought that this style of modern music would be well suited to the inclusive atmosphere of Ubud. So the Jazz Café became Bali's first jazz venue.

The Jazz Café has a unique slogan, "Food for the Soul". The café is open every day except Monday from around 5.30 PM until around midnight. The musicians who play there are from the local community, both Indonesians and expatriates.

The atmosphere of the Jazz Café reminds one of jazz cafés in the United States; the interior is decorated with photos of American jazz musicians such as Louis Armstrong, Billie Holiday, and Dizzy Gillespie. For a cover charge of only Rp 25,000 you can enjoy not only jazz— modern, acid, funk, or acoustic—but sometimes also rhythm and blues, Latin music, or even Beatles covers. It's a very relaxed place where you can eat, drink, and even dance barefoot.

The Jazz Café is a perfect place for people who are used to a bit of night life; the music itself is not too hard or harsh, but gentler music suited to the atmosphere of Ubud.

Figure 6.8 Mozaic

Figure 6.9 Naughty Nuri's

Figure 6.10 Jazz Café

Other restaurants

Apart from those mentioned above, there are plenty of other well-known restaurants in Ubud. One is the Café Lotus, located on Jalan Raya Ubud opposite Pura Taman Kemuda Saraswati (Ubud Water Palace). On certain evenings, the atmosphere here is very dramatic, as we can watch the spectacular performance at the temple while dining in the restaurant. Café Lotus, which opened in 1983, was one of the pioneers among modern restaurants in Ubud.

Another well-known fine-dining restaurant in Ubud is Terazo, on Jalan Suweta. The *Financial Times* of the UK has praised this restaurant owned by Karen Waddell and Ida Bagus Suarsana with the comment "Quality and price that would embarrass your average London restaurateur". This bistro-style restaurant serves Balinese food and wines from France, Italy and Australia, and also features live performances of blues, jazz, and classical music.

Other favorites are Bunute, on Jalan Dewi Sita, and Blue Cat and Warung Opera, both on Jalan Raya Pengosekan. These three places are popular because the celebrated Balinese guitarist Balawan often plays there with his group Batuan Ethnic Fusion[10].

Other excellent restaurants include The Bridge on Jalan Raya Sanggingan, Nomad and Ary's Warung on Jalan Raya Ubud, and Bumbu Bali on Jalan Suweta.

Figure 6.11 Café Lotus

Figure 6.12 Terazo

Figure 6.13 The Bridge

The restaurants listed above are just a small sample of the vast culinary diversity on offer in Ubud. There are other restaurants too numerous to mention serving great food in splendid surroundings, including some in the major hotels in Ubud.

As well as eating in restaurants, we can also sample traditional food in Pasar Ubud or at small roadside food stalls. Along Jalan Raya Sanggingan, for example, near the road heading toward Desa Penestanan, every afternoon there's a stall selling Balinese *sate lilit* made from fish for a shockingly low five hundred rupiah—tasty, wholesome, and amazingly cheap as well.

Figure 6.14 Traditional Food in Pasar Ubud

Figure 6.15 Sate Lilit seller on Jalan Raya Sanggingan

We can see how Ubud has become a paradise for food lovers; almost anything you might want is available. And there's a broad range of atmospheres, from traditional Balinese to European style fine dining ambience.

Interestingly, when a restaurant is full, they will often recommend another place nearby that might be suited to your taste. This indicates a high level of solidarity among the restaurants here. It also shows that the restaurants place top priority on the customers' needs, because by going to another restaurant, the customer does not have to wait too long.

The history of the local restaurant industry is also inspiring, full of tales of successful entrepreneurship. Many of the restaurants, especially the more traditional ones, are run by extended families. This benefits the local economy, because the family members all live in Ubud.

From the business organization perspective, the management of these restaurants is a good example of how a traditional system of business organization based solely on personal trust, with no official, formal commitments, can operate successfully and sustainably.

It's also no coincidence that women have played a major role in founding and managing so many of these restaurants. Traditionally, in Hindu-Bali society, it is the women that prepare the food for religious ceremonies; this is why they don't feel awkward running a culinary business. And since the restaurant employees are also their family members, they are more willing to obey the instructions they are given.

We also see that the owners of these restaurants are not driven simply to reap the greatest possible profits. This is why they don't try to open a lot of branches in other locations, and also why they don't set unreasonable prices. As they see it, running a restaurant business is one form of participation in the cultural development of Ubud.

This is also an aspect of Marketing 3.0: the main focus is not to bring in short-term financial profits, but rather to provide genuine, long-term benefits to all parties concerned.

The management of these restaurants also demonstrates how a brand can become popular without spending much on promotion. Visitors tell other people about these restaurants because they enjoyed them so much; residents who travel outside Ubud tell others because they are so proud of Ubud's restaurants.

The restaurants of Ubud have become a cultural destination in themselves. We enjoy not just the food that is served, but also the atmosphere and the inspiration, as described above. Restaurants in Ubud have become places of spiritual tourism, as they offer a unique, comfortable and sensual ambience where our physical needs are fully satisfied, our knowledge is expanded, and we are spiritually refreshed as well.

(Endnotes)

1 This story of Murni's Warung is taken primarily from the Murni's Warung website, http://www.murnis.com.

2 This story of Warung Babi Guling Ibu Oka is taken primarily from interviews with Anak Agung Oka Sinar and her family.

3 This story of Nasi Ayam Kedewatan Ibu Mangku is taken primarily from an interview with Ibu Mangku.

4 This story of Café Wayan is based mostly on an interview with Mangku Pardita and the Café Wayan brochure.

5 This story of Bebek Bengil is taken primarily from an interview with A.A. Raka Putri, Manager of Bebek Bengil.

6 This story of Indus and Casa Luna is based primarily on a visit to Indus Restaurant and Janet DeNeefe's article "Memories of Casa Luna" published in the Garuda Indonesia in-flight magazine in September 2007.

7 This story of Mozaic Restaurant is taken primarily from the Mozaic website, http://www.mozaic-bali.com.

8 This story of Naughty Nuri's is partly taken from an article by Trisha Sertori, "Make mine the spare ribs and a dry martini" in *The Jakarta Post* on 14 January 2007.

9 This story of the Jazz Café is based mostly on a visit to the restaurant.

10 Balawan, whose full name is I Wayan Balawan, is a Balinese musician born in July 1973. He is known for combining jazz and Balinese gamelan in his compositions, and also for playing a very unusual guitar with two necks, which he plays with an unconventional "tapping" technique similar to playing a piano.

Chapter 7

Natural and Societal Attractions

"The cool natural atmosphere, the panoramas of rice fields, the clear refreshing Oos River, and the simple, straightforward, friendly, people living in harmony—this is the village of Ubud, with all its love."
Dr. Ir. Tjokorda Oka A.A. Sukawati, MSi (Tjok Ace)

The Tri Hita Karana Philosophy[1]

Hindu-Balinese society has a philosophy of life called *Tri Hita Karana*. Literally, Tri Hita Karana means "three sources of happiness" (*tri* = three, *hita* = happiness, *karana* = source). Essentially, this philosophy states that in living our lives in this world, people must maintain harmonious relations on three levels: between humans and God (called "Parahyangan"), between humans and nature ("Palemahan"), and among humans ("Pawongan").

All three of these aspects play critical roles in human life. God created the natural universe and all that it contains, including humans. Nature provides places and substances needed for human life. And people need other people to survive. The relations between these three parties keep the wheels of life turning. If any of these relationships is disrupted, the entire pattern of life will also be disturbed.

All activities in the daily life of the Balinese are guided by the Tri Hita Karana philosophy. Newcomers must also respect and abide by this philosophy while in Bali. Only by implementing Tri Hita Karana can humans achieve peace in this life.

By consistently implementing Tri Hita Karana, Bali's culture, traditions and nature are preserved.

The application of the Tri Hita Karana philosophy can be seen in many places in Ubud. We see that the spiritual, environmental, and social aspects—which are also important elements of Marketing 3.0—are always observed in the management of these places, further strengthening the character and *taksu* of Ubud. Here are brief stories of some of these places.[2]

Pasar Ubud: A Cultural Market

Pasar Ubud is a traditional market that plays an important role in the development and promotion of arts and culture in Ubud. It's not known exactly when this old market, right across the road from Puri Ubud, was established. The current building is the result of renovations completed on 6 October 1994 and inaugurated by the Governor of Bali at the time, Prof. Dr. Ida Bagus Oka.

The market complex comprises a two-story building with a basement area. The basement serves as a traditional market where vegetables and other daily needs are sold. The ground floor and second floor are occupied mostly by traders selling souvenirs intended for tourists. Other traders sell their wares in the interior parking area.

In this market, we can buy many unusual traditional products that are hard to find anywhere else. For example, there's a wide variety of textile products: traditional Balinese clothing, T-shirts with Bali designs, casual unisex pants, Balinese batik, cloth for sarongs, bags, sheets, tablecloths, wall hangings, and blankets with patterns of colorful traditional paintings.

Paintings in a wide range of styles are also for sale here. The quality is just as good as in the galleries, though the painters are less well known. Some painting shops provide certificates of authenticity from the painters.

You'll also find typical Balinese handicrafts such as masks, wooden and stone statues, rattan furniture, picture frames and book covers made from recycled paper, and jewelry—rings, bracelets, necklaces, and earrings made from beads or silver.

Some traders also sell interesting, creative traditional toys, such as bamboo whistles that emit ducklike squawks, miniature gamelan, spinning tops, toy animals made of paper that walk when you pull a string, kites, noisemakers that sound just like thunder, and many more.

There are also shops that sell spices and seasonings—turmeric, galingale, peppercorns, ginger, ginseng, coriander seed and so on. These items may be familiar to Indonesians, but they make interesting souvenirs for foreign tourists.

The products in Pasar Ubud demonstrate the community's love for the environment; nearly everything is made of natural, recyclable or biodegradable materials. The market is also kept very clean.

Because the market is one of the main tourism destinations in Ubud, it's always crowded, especially during holidays. The corridors are a bit cramped, and the tourists have to jostle one another, but that's part of the place's charm, since they may rarely have visited traditional markets before. And the shops are all full of fascinating, creative products, so you never get bored. Foreign tourists also get to learn and practice the art of haggling—something else they might not experience back home.

Before around eight in the morning, Pasar Ubud is a normal traditional market, meeting the daily needs of the local community; it gets full of tourists later, around midday. The market is fairly quiet in the late afternoon, when many of the traders have gone home.

Though most major Asian cities have traditional markets as tourism destinations—Bugis Street in Singapore, the Central Market in Kuala Lumpur, or the Mongkok night market in Hong Kong—Pasar Ubud feels very different. It's not just a venue for commercial transactions, but a part of Ubud's cultural development.

Nearly all the products on sale here are produced by the local community; very few products come from outside Ubud, or outside Bali. Pasar Ubud is also one of the main venues for interaction among the local people of Ubud, and between the local people and visitors from outside Ubud. And here we can observe the changing trends in art, including how outside influences are adapted by the local community.

In the end, once again, Pasar Ubud is not just a center of the people's economy, but also an important part of cultural development in Ubud.

Figure 7.1 Pasar Ubud in the past

Figure 7.2 Pasar Ubud in recent times

Jalan Kajeng: From the People, By the People, For the People

Jalan Kajeng is a small street near Puri Ubud. It's known as an area with low-priced accommodation, and also as a tourist trail, a pleasant place to enjoy the beauties of Ubud on foot (trekking). The road ends at a lovely rice field.

But the most interesting thing is the street itself. This 100-meter-long street is composed of cement tiles roughly one meter square. Each tile has some kind of inscription or picture—whatever the donor desires.

Donors? Yes, most of the funds to build the road came from the local community or visitors. If you want to donate, Rp 150,000 will get you one cement tile, or six for Rp 750,000 (one extra tile as a bonus). The tiles are then inscribed or decorated by the organizing committee as per the donor's wishes. The names of all donors and the amounts they contributed are written on a whiteboard by the side of the road, to ensure financial transparency. This community self-help program is called "Own a Piece of Our Street!"

It's not that the local government lacks sufficient funds; the government has provided funds to repair the road, as part of the National Community Empowerment Program, PNPM Mandiri. But the "Own a Piece of Our Street!" program is an initiative by the local community to maintain Jalan Kajeng as what they call "the living street of memories and thanks".

The donors come from many walks of life—foreign tourists, restaurateurs, hoteliers, and many others. The pictures and inscriptions are also quite varied. Some write the names of their hotels or restaurants; others write declarations of love, or support for Barack Obama.

Here's just a small sample of what we read along Jalan Kajeng: "Murni's Warung Ubud", "Support Balinese Women", "Sarah Palin Nope Sarah Palin", "...Obama Lah Hope Obama Lah...", "Carpe Diem: Frits, Holland – Gaby, Germany, 26 Juli '03", "Tim & Anna Palmer, Honeymoon Bali 2003", "Kami cinta Bali! Phil & Rose, 7-28-03, USA, Kawin 30 years" with a picture of coconut palms, and much more.

Fascinating, isn't it? The personal memories of the donors are immortalized here for all to see.

Jalan Kajeng has long been a popular spot. A well-known Dutch artist named Han Snel[3] used to live here, so the street is also sometimes called Jalan Han Snel. The street is also home to several restaurants and souvenir shops, and an institution called "Threads of Life".

Figure 7.3 Jalan Kajeng

Threads of Life: A Center for Indonesian Textiles[4]

Threads of Life is a center for traditional Indonesian textiles, located on Jalan Kajeng in Ubud. With the slogan "Towards Sustainable Livelihood", this institution's goal is to preserve the traditional handmade textile arts of Indonesia, mostly from Kalimantan, Java, Sulawesi, Bali, Flores, Sumba, and Timor.

The institute was founded in October 1998 by Made Pung, Made Lolet, and a married couple, William Ingram and Jean Howe. They were motivated by their shared concern that the traditional textile arts of Indonesia were slowly becoming extinct. In 1998, the economic crisis forced many families to sell off their heirloom textiles just to survive. Yet these traditional textiles are quite rare, and can take years to make.

So Threads of Life began collecting these traditional textiles. The institution also studies and teaches the traditional methods of weaving and natural dyeing. The goal is not simply to preserve the products, but also to perpetuate their production methods. Threads of Life also seeks to discover the history and significance behind the making of each style of traditional textile.

The institute conducts many activities: classes and workshops on various aspects of textiles, and occasional exhibitions. Threads of Life also conducts women's empowerment activities, because women play the major role in producing traditional textiles.

Threads of Life is making a serious effort to preserve local cultures, because traditional textiles are an essential part of culture that gets passed on from generation to generation.

Figure 7.4 Threads of Life

Desa Penestanan: The Artists' Village

One village in Ubud, Desa Penestanan, is known as a center for artists. Many of the residents were students of Arie Smit and therefore paint in a style somewhat similar to his, called the "Young Artists" style (see Chapter 3). Here we can find many working studios and galleries displaying works of these Young Artists.

The village lies to the west of Jalan Raya Sanggingan. There are two ways to get there. If you have a motor vehicle, you can take the steep road that starts next to Museum Blanco. If you're on foot, there's a trail of steep steps, around 100 meters north of the road.

At the trailhead of this stairway, there are a number of name boards announcing the various accommodations in Desa Penestanan. As well as being an artists' community, the village is also known for its low-cost lodgings. Many of these are local people's homes that have been slightly modified to serve as home stays for tourists. But there are several luxurious hotels and resorts here as well.

By the sides of the stairway are statues, with names carved into them—Brooke, Anne, Terry, and so on. Apparently these are names of donors who contributed to build the stairway, as in Jalan Kajeng.

Desa Penestanan is also famous as one of Bali's beadwork centers. In several spots, you will find craftspersons producing items decorated with beads—earthenware, ceramics, bracelets, necklaces, bags and so on. The village is also known for nature tourism, as it has broad rice fields with lovely panoramas.

With all these attractions—home studios of painters and handicraft producers, cheap accommodation, and nature—Desa Penestanan is one of the most interesting destinations in Ubud.

Figure 7.5 Desa Penestanan

The Monkey Forest: A Monkey Sanctuary[5]

One place no visitor to Ubud should miss is the Sacred Monkey Forest Sanctuary (Mandala Wisata Wenara Wana), usually just called the Monkey Forest. As the name suggests, it is home to around 300 long-tailed macaques (*Macaca fascicularis*).

Since it's a natural forest, this nine-hectare area is full of trees and other forms of wildlife; there's also a deer breeding center. It's a very pleasant place for families; you'll see many people taking their young children to visit the Monkey Forest.

On the left and the right of the main entrance gate to the Monkey Forest are two giant statues of monkeys, and at the boundary of the tourism forest are two giant statues of *resi*, mystic priests. Occasionally people place small offerings, *canang*, before the resi statues and offer brief prayers. Usually when the worshippers leave, monkeys come and eat the offerings.

The monkeys in the forest are considered sacred. Even when they eat offerings, or wander beyond the boundaries of the forests toward local people's homes, nobody bothers them or chases them away.

This demonstrates respect for the monkeys, as fellow creatures of God. They are allowed to roam freely wherever they want. But the monkeys seldom stray very far from the forest, normally only as far as the road or the nearest houses.

Because they are used to seeing humans, the monkeys seem tame, though they are not caged. They don't seem to be bothered by the presence of visitors, who may number hundreds each day. But occasionally their animal nature gets the better of them; they do sometimes take food from tourists, or other things that attract their attention—glasses or jewelry, for example—so visitors have to be on guard. On the other hand, don't worry too much, because as long as you don't disturb them, they're unlikely to bother you. And there are personnel on hand to deal with any problematic interspecies interactions.

The Monkey Forest also contains three temples: Pura Dalem Agung, Pura Prajapati, and Pura Mandi Suci, which were built in the 14th century. The local people consider the monkeys living in the forest as the protectors of these temples.

Pura Dalem Agung is the main temple, to honor Dewa Siwa; Pura Prajapati is to honor Dewi Durga, his consort. These temples contain a crematorium and a burial place for human remains that have not yet been cremated.[6]

The other temple, Pura Mandi Suci (Holy Bathing Temple), has, as its name indicates, a pool of water that is considered holy. Pura Mandi Suci is rather far downhill; to get there, you have to pass through the roots of an ancient banyan tree. There's also a stone statue of a komodo dragon, covered with green moss.

Traditional religious ceremonies are occasionally held in the Monkey Forest, called Tumpek Kandang and Tumpek Nguduh. The Tumpek Kandang ceremony is to honor the monkeys and other animals, while Tumpek Nguduh is to honor the plants in the Monkey Forest.

So, unlike many other forest areas, where the only activities are purely for forest conservation, the Monkey Forest is full of other activities. We have interaction between humankind and God through the religious ceremonies at the temples; interaction between humans, when the local people perform these ceremonies, and among the visitors to the Forest; and the forest itself is a place where humans interact with nature.

Figure 7.6 Monkey Forest

Desa Kokokan: The White Heron Sanctuary

Another nature tourism destination with unusual animals is Desa Petulu, also often called Desa Kokokan. This village is around three kilometers north of Pasar Ubud, on the way to Tegallalang. Unlike the

Monkey Forest, Desa Kokokan is not a specially designated zone, but just an ordinary village.

It's called Desa Kokokan because it is home to over 15,000 white herons (in Balinese, *kokokan*). The birds fly from tree to tree, or perch on top of people's homes or along the village road. Because there are so many of them, the whole area—roads, trees, rice fields, rooftops—is white with their droppings and feathers.

In the morning, we can see great flocks of herons flying off to seek food all over the island of Bali, and in the late afternoon we see these same thousands of birds returning to their nests after a day of feeding. So the best times to visit are early morning and late afternoon, when the birds are in flight; there aren't many birds here in the middle of the day.

In the middle of the rice fields is a simple warung, the most strategic place to watch the birds flying to or from their nests. Near the warung is a three-sided wooden pillar inscribed "Semoga Damai di Indonesia", "Semoga Damai di Dunia", and "May Peace Prevail on Earth".

Apparently, the herons all arrived in Desa Petulu in a great mass in November 1965. Nobody knows where they came from. They arrived shortly after the community of Desa Petulu had held a series of ceremonies to beseech God to grant them a better life. And indeed, after the birds came, the village's economy gradually improved. For this reason, the local people consider the birds sacred and never disturb them, and hunting them would be completely out of the question.

As a unique tourism venue that conserves a rare bird species, Desa Kokokan received the Kalpataru award from the Indonesian government in 1991.

Figure 7.7 Desa Kokokan

Bali Bird Walks[7]

Bali Bird Walks is just that—a tour program where we can walk through the rice fields of Ubud and observe the various bird species. The program has been operated since 1990 by its initiators, Victor Mason and Wayan Sumadi. Mason is a British ornithologist who has lived in Ubud for many years. He has also written a book by the same name, *Bali Bird Walks*.

The tours are conducted every Tuesday, Friday, Saturday and Sunday from 9.00 AM to 12.30 PM, starting from a spot called Beggar's Bush, on Jalan Raya Sanggingan opposite Museum Blanco.

On your walk, you're sure to see at least 30 of the 100 bird species in Ubud, as well as many species of butterflies and plants in and around the green rice fields and leafy coconut trees.

During the walks, Mason often goes barefoot; it's actually more comfortable that way, once you're used to it. Tour participants are equipped with binoculars to see the birds more clearly. Participants are also given a list of birds to enable them to identify what they see.

This program is great fun for children, as they can enjoy an adventure in the great outdoors and see many beautiful species of birds. Tour participants also often encounter local residents and schoolchildren, because the route also passes through residential areas. So as well as interacting with nature, participants also get to interact with the local people.

Figure 7.8 Bali Bird Walks

The Tjampuhan Hills: A Nature Walk Adventure

One very historic area is the Tjampuhan hills, along the banks of the Oos River. Winding through these hills is a footpath that local residents used to take to get to the Puri Ubud area in the days before there were motor vehicles here. This trail, now known as the Tjampuhan Ridge Path, starts at Pura Gunung Lebah and ends at Desa Bangkiang Sidem in North Ubud.

This is the path that children from North Ubud had to take to get to school, motivating the King of Ubud, Tjokorda Gde Agung Sukawati, to build schools in Ubud (see Chapter 2). It was also the path people used when they wanted to trade or shop at Pasar Ubud, or attend ceremonies at Pura Gunung Lebah.

Nowadays, the trail through the Tjampuhan hills is mostly used for trekking and jogging, as the air is very fresh. Some people also walk their dogs there. You'll also see local people cutting the tall grass to use as animal feed. And quite a few young people use the area for romantic encounters, so another name for it is "Bukit Cinta", Love Hill.

The panoramas along this trail are truly stunning. The trail is paved with a sort of brick tiles and surrounded by high elephant grass (*ilalang*). We can also see virgin forest along the river banks and, across the river, the hotels and villas along Jalan Raya Sanggingan. The ambience is even more beautiful just before sunset, when the fading sunlight creates a surreal, mysterious atmosphere, giving the place yet another name, "Sunset Hill".

Walking through the hills is most pleasant in the morning or late afternoon, when the sun is less intense. The hike takes around two or three hours, depending on how fast you walk and what you do along the way.

At the end of the trail, we come to Desa Bangkiang Sidem, which has an art gallery and restaurant called Klub Kokos. There's also a road that motor vehicles can use, so if you're really exhausted, you can get a lift from here back to the main part of Ubud. Or if you're not worn out yet, you can continue northward on foot through Desa Payogan until you reach Jalan Lungsiakan.

Along the way to Jalan Lungsiakan, we pass through residential areas, rice fields, and home gardens. You may see painters at work in their homes, including egg painters. Also on this part of the trail is Pura Pucak Payogan, in Desa Pakraman Lungsiakan.

The trail is twisty and has many ups and downs; after all, it is in the hills. It's very tranquil, with just one or two motor vehicles passing by. Occasionally you meet village children out for a stroll.

The hike may be tiring, but we still feel physically, emotionally and spiritually refreshed both during and after our trek along this historic trail.

Figure 7.9 The Tjampuhan Hills

Ubud Botanic Garden: A Garden of Vision[8]

The Ubud Botanic Garden is in Desa Kutuh Kaja, North Ubud, around 2½ km from Pasar Ubud. This four-hectare garden is run not by the government, but by the private sector. It was developed by Stefan Reisner from Germany and Faizah from Surabaya starting in February 2005 and opened on 15 June 2006. Later, in 2007, Herta Falkenburg from Austria/ South Africa joined as their partner.

The Ubud Botanic Garden has an interesting history. In his younger days, Stefan Reisner was a novelist and dramatist. He then worked as a journalist for *Stern* magazine, serving as their foreign correspondent in Hong Kong for 12 years. Then, in 1998, he moved to Bali and started the Hotel Puri Asri.

While operating the hotel, Stefan was often asked by guests if there was a tropical garden to visit somewhere in Bali. He was therefore inspired to build a garden like the Royal Gardens in Potsdam and in his home town, Berlin. Stefan sold his hotel and, together with Faizah, rented the land that has now become the Ubud Botanic Garden. Faizah is an orchid lover and the former owner of a hotel in Desa Petulu. Originally from Surabaya, Faizah worked in Jakarta for 12 years and moved to Bali in 1998.

They started the Ubud Botanic Garden to foster love for and better understanding of the natural environment and to protect plant species found in the tropics, especially in Bali. The collection also includes plants from Sumatra, Kalimantan, Papua, and Sulawesi.

The garden is theme-based, with several areas: Pitcher Plants, Bamboo Garden, Helikonia Hill, Meditation Court, Rain Forest, Orchid House, Herbal Garden, Islam Garden, Labyrinth, Love Nest, Succulents, and Bromeliad Garden.

In the Pitcher Plants area, we see tropical carnivorous plants that are brightly colored to attract insects and other small animals. Once an animal become trapped in the pitcher-shaped flower, the plant's leaves close in on it, and its fluids impede the victim's escape. Slowly, the unfortunate creature drowns and is digested by the plant.

Another interesting area is the Meditation Court, a rather small area that is ideal for meditation, as it is surrounded by rock walls and dense forest, making it very peaceful and relaxing. There's also a small temple. But it's not restricted to Hindu-Balinese; it's open to anyone who wants to come and meditate.

There's also a small labyrinth, perhaps the only one in Bali. The labyrinth is made up of tall, dense shrubs. In Hindu-Balinese belief, a labyrinth is a challenge to the thoughts and spirit of those who enter it. It's believed that a pregnant woman who is able to exit the labyrinth will have an easy delivery.

The Ubud Botanic Garden is a great place for families. We learn a lot about plants, and we are physically and spiritually refreshed by the fresh air and our adventure in this calm, leafy place.

As Stefan Reisner says about the garden, "Travelers can come to a standstill after thousands of miles of noisy travel…Our Botanic Garden is like a palace with the sky as roof and many different rooms, secret chambers, galleries and staircases. The visitor wanders through changing vistas and experiences, encouraged to trespass into Nature. This is the message of our Garden."

Figure 7.10 Ubud Botanic Garden

Ubud Organic Market: Back to Nature

In the past few years, organic foods have become increasingly popular around the world. Organic food is seen as the solution to health problems in the human body, and also as a cure for the "health" of Planet Earth[9].

Many restaurants and shops in Ubud sell natural food, and other organic products as well. These organic foods and products are grown by local farmers and by expatriates who live in Ubud.

The community of producers and consumers of organic food regularly gathers at the Ubud Organic Market. This small market meets in the courtyard of Pizza Bagus restaurant on Raya Pengosekan, near Museum ARMA, and is only open on Saturdays from 9.30 AM to 2.00 PM.

There's a huge variety of organic food products on sale: fresh fruit and vegetables, basic foodstuffs such as rice, many types of bread and cakes, syrup, juice, yogurt, and home-made jams and salad dressings. Other stalls sell medicinal plants and herbal remedies, such as *tapak dewa, mahkota dewa, kumis kucing,* and *temulawak.*

The Ubud Organic Market also has non-food organic products such as body care products, including liquid soap, toothpaste, herbal bath preparations, and body lotion. Also available are bleaching salt and natural mosquito-repelling incense. Other stalls sell products for health therapy and meditation, such as virgin coconut oil, ylang-ylang flower powder for meditation, therapeutic candles, and aromatherapy salts.

Also sold in the market are soap nuts (*klerek* or *lerak*), a natural cleaning agent. Sold in ½-kg and 1-kg packages, klerek is used by the traditional community to wash all kinds of things—plants, batik and other clothing, gold and silver jewelry, and as a dandruff shampoo. Because of these many benefits, klerek is often called "natural magic soap".

The organic products bought and sold in the market come not only from Ubud and Bali; some are from other regions of Indonesia or even from abroad, such as Monggo chocolate bars from Yogyakarta and royal jelly and royal ginseng products from China.

To carry away your purchases, vendors supply cloth bags that can be used over and over again, as an ecologically sound alternative to plastic bags. Some shoppers bring their own bags made from old newspapers.

As well as helping to protect the environment, this organic community also empowers the local economy. The Ubud Organic

Market was started to help the local community, organic farmers, and small traders to survive self-sufficiently. The slogan here is "Fair Trade", as opposed to "Free Trade", which is seen as advantageous only to global businesses from large countries.

The Ubud Organic Market is an interesting example of how global influences that are in harmony with local values can flourish in Ubud. Without realizing it, the people of Ubud were already producing and consuming what the outside world refers to as "organic" food and products. So when the newcomers repackaged these goods with the name "organic," the people of Ubud accepted them immediately.

Figure 7.11 Ubud Organic Market

Pondok Pekak[10]

Another place that embodies Ubud's Tri Hita Karana philosophy is Pondok Pekak or, to use its full name, the "Pondok Pekak Library & Learning Centre". As well as being a library, it's also an art studio and a learning center for the local community.

Pondok Pekak, located next to the Ubud Football Field, is not very big, only around 100 square meters, with two stories. It was started by a married couple, Made Sumendra and Laurie Billington. Laurie is an American expatriate who enjoys reading and has a vision that every city has to have a library. So, with the support of her husband and his family, she started the Pondok Pekak library in their home in 1995.

The name "Pondok Pekak" means "Grandpa's Place" (*pekak* is Balinese for "grandfather"). They gave it this name to honor the family's grandfather, Pekak Mangku, who is also an avid reader, a *pedande* (priest), a healer, and a respected village elder.

The library at Pondok Pekak has a collection of over 10,000 books in several languages. They also offer various courses: wood carving, painting, dance, music, *banten* making, silverwork, fruit handicrafts, bamboo weaving, and so on. The place is also used by expatriates to study Bahasa Indonesia, as it's a very conducive venue for learning.

There's also a small stage, used for cultural performances by children. The children include not only kids from the local community, but also the children of expatriates living in Ubud. Posted on one notice board is what they call the "World Peace Map", a map made by children from bits of cardboard in various shapes and sizes, all pasted on to form a map of the world.

With the theme "Let's Make a Peaceful World Together!", the children have written some of their hopes on the pieces of cardboard. These messages include "Joy! Be Happy and Others will Follow Your Lead! Smile!", "Sing Ken Ken", "Help Each Other", "I Love Mom", "Love Save the Earth", and the like.

It's interesting, isn't it, how the children are being introduced to these humanitarian ideas. This is in line with Pondok Pekak's slogan, "Promoting peace through reading, literacy and education". From a very early age, the children here are taught to respect others, despite differences in culture, nationality and language.

Figure 7.12 Pondok Pekak

Pelangi School[11]

Pelangi School is a community school, founded by expatriates living in Ubud to educate their children at a school with international standards. Previously, the only such schools were in Badung Regency, in Kuta, Legian, Sanur, and Nusa Dua, quite far from Ubud. So there was a strong motivation to establish Pelangi School.

The school, opened in July 2006, is in Desa Kumbuh, on the southern borders of Ubud. The curriculum used here combines the Indonesian national curriculum and the British national curriculum. The levels offered start with Tiny Tots, continuing through Playgroup, Kindergarten A and B to Primary School (Grades 1–6). Instruction is bilingual, in English and Indonesian.

As well as teaching academic knowledge, Pelangi School also seeks to inculcate in its pupils social and environmental awareness and to guide their social, emotional, moral, intellectual, physical, and artistic development. This is referred to as Holistic Education—multicultural, creative and student-centered.

Though there were only a few students in the first year, now there are over 80, and not all are from the expatriate community; there are local children as well. Another interesting program run by Yayasan Cahaya Pelangi is a "daily drop-in" for children of tourists who are visiting Ubud. Parents can drop their children off to play and learn with their age-mates at the school while they go sightseeing in Ubud.

Pelangi School also provides scholarships for students from disadvantaged families. The funds come from donations, fund-raising events, and sales at the Pelangi Shop in Pengosekan. In 2008, the scholarship fund came to Rp 150 million.

The name *pelangi* means "rainbow", and the school is indeed a perfect place to educate children from the start about the importance of living together in peace, harmony and mutual respect in a world that is diverse not just culturally but also in terms of economic status.

Figure 7.13 Pelangi School

IDEP Foundation: Empowering Local Communities[12]

One example of a foundation or non-governmental organization that plays an active role in empowering local communities is Yayasan IDEP (IDEP Foundation). IDEP stands for Indonesian Development of Education and Permaculture.

Yayasan IDEP, on Jalan Hanoman, was founded in 1999 when Indonesia was suffering a severe economic crisis. The foundation's programs can be broadly grouped into four categories: environmental programs, educational programs, community development programs, and disaster management programs.

One feature that differentiates Yayasan IDEP from other similar organizations is its disaster management programs. IDEP conducts community-based disaster management activities at every stage of disasters: community preparedness, emergency response, and sustainable recovery.

In managing disasters, the Foundation sets a target of being on the scene no longer than 36 hours after a disaster strikes, in the critical period when aid is most urgently needed. The Foundation played a major role in handling the emergencies created by the Bali bombings in 2002 and 2005 and in aiding disaster victims after the tsunami in Aceh. IDEP raised and delivered over US$1 million to assist tsunami victims in Aceh.

Apart from the disaster management program, another unique program is Permaculture education. "Permaculture" is an abbreviation for "Permanent Agriculture and Permanent Culture", a term coined by Bill Mollison and David Holmgren in the 1970s.

The objective of permaculture is to design harmonious integration of landscape and people to provide food, shelter, energy and other material or non-material needs in a sustainable way. Permaculture is a holistic concept that integrates traditional practices of earth stewardship with appropriate uses of modern technology. (Sounds like another application of the Tri Hita Karana philosophy, doesn't it?)

Yayasan IDEP has conducted Permaculture training for over 200 people since 1999, and various Permaculture projects have been conducted in places throughout Indonesia.

Another important program run by IDEP is "Bali Cares". Bali Cares is a non-profit project started in 2004 to assist local charitable organizations.

Bali Cares has a shop located next to the Yayasan IDEP office, selling handicrafts, food products, health products, postcards, and bookmarks. All the products come from the local community and help to enhance their prosperity, in line with the Bali Cares slogan, "Every purchase makes a difference in someone's life".

The story of the IDEP Foundation shows that the Tri Hita Karana philosophy is now being understood and applied by a broader community in Ubud, not just the Hindu-Balinese, though these other community groups might not even realize this.

Figure 7.14 IDEP Foundation

Apart from the places and institutions described above, there are many other examples of the Tri Hita Karana philosophy applied in practice in Ubud. One such example is the I Dewa Nyoman Batuan Artists Community in Pengosekan. This comvmunity, founded in 1970, popularized paintings of flora and fauna, which came to be known as the Pengosekan Style. Through this community, artists can work together and exchange their ideas in developing their art works.

Figure 7.15 I Dewa Nyoman Batuan Artists Community in Pengosekan

Another example is the training in modern environmental management techniques—waste management, water management, reforestation, and ecobuilding—conducted by several institutions in Ubud. Many places also offer recycled products: name cards, brochures, bags and packages.

This environmental awareness can even be seen in a sign posted on the grass outside Ubud State Junior High School 1 on Jalan Raya Ubud, across from Museum Puri Lukisan, which reads (in translation) "Love Me as You Love Yourself".

There's also the "Books for Bali" project supported by Ganesha Bookshop in Ubud. The project collects books and donates them to local libraries and schools to encourage local children, and the entire community, to develop the reading habit and motivate them to learn.

All these stories show that the people of Ubud really care for their environment, including animals and plants, with all their hearts. Ubud's community also maintains a strong sense of internal solidarity, which enables them to perform many development activities by themselves.

This consistent and integrated application of the Tri Hita Karana philosophy is what gives Ubud its intense taksu, which just keeps on getting stronger.

(Endnotes)

1   This explanation of the Tri Hita karana philosophy comes from interviews with Tjok Putra (Drs. Tjokorda Gde Putra Sukawati) and Tjok 'De (Drs. Tjokorda Gde Raka Sukawati MM), among other sources.

2   The stories of these places are based mostly on visits to the places concerned.

3   Han Snel was born in the Netherlands on 16 July 1925. He lived on Jalan Kajeng starting in the 1950s and died in Ubud on 26 May 1998. Han Snel was known for a painting style called "roundism". His former home is still there, now called the Han Snel Home Stay or Siti's Bungalow, after Han's wife.

4   This description of Threads of Life comes from the Threads of Life brochure and the Threads of Life website, http://www.threadsoflife.com.

5   This story of the Monkey Forest is based on visits, supplemented by information from the Monkey Forest's brochure and its website, http://www.monkeyforestubud.com.

6   The bodies of Hindu-Balinese who die are not cremated immediately. For more on this, see Chapter 5.

7   This story of Bali Bird Walks is based on visits and on the Bali Bird Walks brochure and its website, http://www.balibirdwalk.com.

8   This story of Ubud Botanic Garden is based on visits, supplemented with information from the Ubud Botanic Garden website, http://www.botanicgardenbali.com.

9   Organic food is defined as food derived from plants or animals grown without the use of chemicals such as pesticides, chemical fertilizers, hormones or antibiotics. This food is typically lower in fat and higher in fiber and protein. Organic crops grown by local farmers can also reduce the air pollution generated by transportation of products.

10   This story of Pondok Pekak is based on visits, supplemented by information from Pondok Pekak's brochure.

11   This story of Pelangi School comes from the Pelangi School website, http://www.pelangischoolbali.com.

12   This story of Yayasan IDEP is based on visits, supplemented by information from the IDEP brochure and the IDEP website, http://www.idepfoundation.org.

Chapter 8

From Ubud for the World

"With its open elite, the festive atmosphere of its dances and rituals, its friendly population and dazzling landscapes, Ubud possessed everything necessary to seduce outside visitors."
Dr. Jean Couteau

Ubud is a city-village that has been the resting place and the home of people from many countries and nationalities. Ubud has, therefore, inevitably been influenced by cultural trends occurring in many parts of the world. These influences can be seen, for example, from the international conferences and events held here, and the emergence of many healing treatment facilities in Ubud.

These outside influences are now entering Ubud even more quickly and easily with the recent advances in technology, particularly telecommunications and the Internet. The flow of information and human interaction is no longer limited by time and space. The world community now knows almost immediately whatever is happening in Ubud. And these technological advances have made it easier for people to cooperate in the various activities conducted in Ubud.

To examine how these technological influences have enabled people to know what's going on in Ubud and to work together in conducting activities in Ubud, let's look briefly at two of the world's most popular Internet sites: YouTube and Facebook.

When we accessed YouTube on 18 August 2009, there were more than 2000 video clips on Ubud, averaging less than three minutes in duration. The content was varied: the atmosphere at Pasar Ubud, dance performances, the scene in people's accommodations, Warung Babi Guling Ibu Oka, the Monkey Forest, a brief profile of I Gusti Nyoman Lempad, and much more.

On Facebook, on the same date, there were over 22 pages, 100 groups, and 108 events related to Ubud. The topics being discussed included the Ubud Writers & Readers Festival, painting exhibitions, information on lodgings in Ubud, photography, and many others.

From all this information available in online media, people can learn a lot about Ubud, even if they've never been there. Furthermore, all this interaction in online media eventually creates an online community related to Ubud. This online community can then develop into an offline community when its members meet in person. Conversely, the existing offline community can work and develop more rapidly by using online media.

Thus, it's not surprising that within the last decade or so, many international-scale events have been held in Ubud. And these programs have, to a lesser or greater extent, influenced contemporary cultural trends within Ubud. Through these international events, Ubud has also become known as a unique venue for MICE (Meetings, Incentives, Conventions, Exhibitions). Below, we describe a few of these programs.

Ubud Writers & Readers Festival[1]

The Ubud Writers & Readers Festival was conceived by Janet DeNeefe, owner of Indus and Casa Luna restaurants, author of the book *Fragrant Rice* and columnist in the Garuda Indonesia in-flight magazine (see Chapter 6). The Festival is organized by a foundation called Yayasan Mudra Swari Saraswati (or simply Yayasan Saraswati), also founded by Janet DeNeefe and her husband, Ketut Suardana.

The Festival was created as a response to the damaging impact of the first Bali bombing on 12 October 2002. At that time, the image of Bali was in terrible shape; many people were afraid to visit Bali. Janet came up with the idea of holding an international-scale event to help restore Bali's image and encourage people not to be afraid of visiting.

The first Ubud Writers & Readers Festival was held in 2004, and it has been held routinely every year since them. The Festival is a forum that brings together writers, publishers, and lovers of literature from around the world to exchange their thoughts on a wide range of current topics—everything from literature and language to religion, the environment, lifestyle, and human rights.

Because of this important role, this festival has received international recognition, acclaimed as "one of the world's great book festivals" by *Condé Nast Travel and Leisure* magazine, and "among the top six literary festivals in the world" by *Harper's Bazaar* from the UK.

In addition to discussions, the Festival features many other events: book launches, readings, cultural and musical performances, literary lunches and dinners, cocktail parties, writing and cultural workshops, and art exhibits. There's even a workshop program for children.

Speakers at the Festival come from many countries. Among those who have attended in previous years are Richard Flanagan from Australia, Vikram Seth from India, John Berendt from the US, Yan Geling from China, Alberto Ruy-Sanchez from Mexico, Bernice Chauly from Malaysia, and 2007 Man Booker Prize short-listed writer Indra Sinha from the UK.

From Indonesia, Bondan Winarno, Debra Yatim, and Andrea Hirata are among the many who have taken part in the Festival. Andrea Hirata, the Indonesian writing phenomenon whose *Laskar Pelangi* series of books has sold hundreds of thousands of copies, appeared in 2008 to discuss his novel *Maryamah Karpov*, which was just about to be published.

We can see how this festival has become a vehicle for interaction across cultures and across generations. For the society of Bali, and Indonesia as a whole, the Festival has brought significant benefits by being a means to foster cooperation among writers and a forum to introduce young Indonesian writers.

The Ubud Writers & Readers Festival has a different theme each year, always referring to some aspect of Hindu-Balinese philosophy.

In 2007, the theme was "*Skala-Niskala*: The Seen and the Unseen", and in 2008, "*Tri Hita Karana*". For the sixth festival in 2009, the theme is "*Suka Duka*: Compassion and Solidarity"[2].

The festival is attended not only by writers; many others come and take part in the various activities—diplomats, artists and art lovers, cultural figures, academics, executives, and the general public. Several activities are going on at any one time, giving participants the opportunity to attend whichever program most interests them. As Debra H. Yatim says in the Festival's Facebook account, "The Festival was wonderful; we were like children in a candy shop not knowing which lollipop to choose".

Through the Festival, Ubud has become better known to the world. The Ubud Writers & Readers Festival has also enhanced the development of Ubud's character. Previously, Ubud was best known for its painters; now, with this festival, Ubud is also known as a place of inspiration for writers from around the world.

Figure 8.1 Ubud Writers & Readers Festival (courtesy of the Festival committee)

Bali Institute for Global Renewal/Quest for Global Healing Conferences[3]

Another international forum held in Ubud is the Quest for Global Healing Conferences, now known as the Bali Institute for Global Renewal.

This forum was established by Marcia Jaffe, an organizer of meetings and international conferences with over 30 years experience. While on holiday in Bali in late 2003, Jaffe was inspired to hold a conference in Bali to discuss global problems such as leadership, peace, spirituality, humanity, poverty, and culture. The basic objective of the conference was to "heal the Earth" and the humans who live on it.

From this idea, the Quest for Global Healing Conference was held in 2004, followed by the Quest for Global Healing Conference II in 2006. At the third conference in August 2007, the Bali Institute for Global Renewal (usually simply called the "Bali Institute") was founded.

Jaffe also has a home in Sausalito, at the end of the Golden Gate Bridge in the San Francisco Bay Area. She spends half her time in Ubud and the other half in Sausalito, and the Bali Institute has offices in both places.

While the first two conferences were focused mostly on dialogue and training, with the establishment of the Bali Institute, the participants focus more on action they can actually take. Ideas should not stop at the discussion level, but should be realized concretely by the participants when they return home, in line with their newly enhanced capacities.

The Bali Institute is a world learning center aimed at empowering individuals and organizations in their quest to make a difference in the world and bring about cross-cultural understanding and world peace. The Institute comprises a consortium of international organizations, companies, NGOs, universities, consultants, and thought leaders from around the world.

Because it comes from Bali, the Bali Institute seeks to introduce the living culture of Bali to the world and to take inspiration from Bali's culture as an alternative solution to overcome the world's problems. The

Bali Institute's mission is to serve as a vehicle for the world community to exchange ideas; like a *banjar*, but on a global level.

Jaffe says that cross-border, cross-cultural and cross-generation activities like those the Institute conducts are becoming more frequent all over the world.

The three conferences held in 2004, 2006, and 2007 were attended by thousands of people from dozens of countries and highly diverse backgrounds—university students, cultural figures, executives, and non-governmental organizations—and of all ages, from very young to very senior. All of them seek to play a role in effecting social change and feel that Bali is a part of their personal transformational experiences.

Participants also have the rare opportunity to engage in personal dialogues with world leaders. For example, the Quest for Global Healing Conference II in 2006 at Museum ARMA was attended by three Nobel Peace Prize winners: Archbishop Desmond Tutu, Betty Williams, and Jody Williams; Edgar Mitchell, former Apollo 14 astronaut and the sixth person to walk on the moon; and former Indonesian President Abdurrahman Wahid.

Bali, and especially Ubud, is an ideal place to discuss the problems plaguing the world today and to seek solutions to these problems. As Marcia Jaffe says, "Bali and its culture serve as a vitally important container for exploring global issues and learning how to heal, forgive, and live harmoniously with one another and the planet".

Figure 8.2 Global Healing Conferences (courtesy of the Conferences committee)

Balispirit Festival[4]

The Balispirit Festival is a festival aimed at developing spirituality through yoga, dance, and music. The Festival was conceived by a couple, I Made Gunarta and Meghan Pappenheim, who were inspired by the "world music" concepts of American musician Rob Weber. Made and Meghan decided to hold an event that was more than just a music festival—a more complete activity also encompassing yoga, spirituality, and dance performances from various cultures around the world.

Through this festival, talented yogis, dancers and musicians from Bali and Indonesia get the chance to display their skills. At the same time, yogis, dancers and musicians from all parts of the world come and share their experiences. Ultimately, the Festival is aimed at helping the participants to create positive changes in the world around them.

The Festival was first held in 2008 at the Purnati Centre for the Arts in Ubud. Only a few people, from Indonesia and abroad, were involved in arranging it, and all the funding came from the Festival's founders. Nevertheless, the first Festival was a success and was endorsed by the Bali Tourism Board.

Because the first Festival was such a success, for the second Festival in 2009, the Balispirit Festival applied more professional management, with a more complete and more experienced team. The Festival was also supported in various ways by a number of government institutions, mass media, and companies.

During the Festival, participants can take part in various yoga and meditation classes and workshops or watch world-class dance and music performances. The participants come from many backgrounds: yogis, dancers, musicians, backpackers, executives, and people from the general public who are interested by the Festival's activities.

The instructors and performers come from many countries. For yoga, they have included Swami Shankardev Saraswati from Australia, Katy Appleton from the UK, Ravindranath Vempati from India, Mark Whitwell from New Zealand, Joseph Lee from Singapore, and many others.

Dance instructors and performers have included Akiko Tokuoka from Jepang, Pooja Bhatnagar from India, Akim Funk Buddha from the U.S., Sibo Bangoura from West Africa, and many others. Foreign musicians taking part include Mia Palencia from Malaysia, Rocky Dawuni from Ghana, Ganga Giri from Australia, Daphne Tse from the U.S., and Khalife from Lebanon.

From Indonesia, instructors and performers have included Merta Ada, Pujiastuti Sindhu, I Wayan Marcus Wistika, and Kadek Suambara for yoga, Ni Ketut Arini and Maria Darmaningsih for dance, and musicians Slamet Gundono, Simak Dialog, and Saharadja.

The Balispirit Festival is perhaps the first festival of its kind, combining yoga, dance, and music as a way to develop humankind's inner spirituality. It is this spirituality within each of us that will ultimately provide solutions to the world's problems. As one participant, Afro-American musician Michael Franti, says, "Come (to Balispirit Festival) and be a part of the healing of the planet!"

Figure 8.3 Balispirit Festival (courtesy of the Festival committee)

Yoga: The Traditional Practice of Meditation

One method used by many people in Ubud to develop their inner spirituality is yoga. Many yoga-related facilities and activities have emerged in the past five years or so, including the Balispirit Festival.

Briefly, yoga is a traditional healing practice originally from India. Yoga practices include movement, breathing, and relaxation techniques.

The word *yoga* comes from Sanskrit and means "to yoke", "to unite" or "to control". In other words, by practicing yoga a person can reunite all the parts of his/her body, thoughts, breath and spirit that have become separated because of the various activities we engage in. After performing yoga, our thoughts are calm, our spirits refreshed, and our bodies healthy.

Yoga and meditation—though perhaps in different forms—have been practiced in Ubud since the earliest times. You will probably remember from Chapter 2 that Rsi Markandya meditated in many places while exploring and founding Ubud.

And because it shares cultural roots with the values so long upheld by the society of Ubud, yoga has grown here quite rapidly. Ubud now has many facilities and shops offering various products related to yoga and meditation, for example the Yoga Barn on Jalan Raya Pengosekan and the Meditation Shop and Intuitive Flow in Desa Penestanan. Yoga programs are also offered in many places in Ubud, at all levels from absolute beginner to highly advanced.

Ubud's atmosphere is ideally conducive to activities such as yoga and meditation. The air is fresher and the ambience calmer than in most other parts of Bali, and certainly more spiritual, so Ubud is a perfect place for introspection and contemplation.

By doing yoga, a person gains not only improved physical fitness but also a sense of happiness, joy and inner satisfaction.

The health thereby obtained is holistic wellbeing, which in turn encourages positive changes in lifestyle.

Figure 8.4 Yoga practice in Ubud (courtesy of the Balispirit Festival committee)

Humanitad Foundation[5]

The Humanitad Foundation was founded in 1999 by Sacha Adams Stone, a British citizen born in Rhodesia (now Zimbabwe). Humanitad is an international, non-government, non-profit organization dedicated to promoting unity among the nations, faiths and cultures on earth through the conception and realization of projects and activities that celebrate the unity of humankind.

Sacha, with his long, curly hair, was formerly a rock musician with the Purple Angels and Stone. He is an Anglican, but has studied many religions and faiths during his travels around the world. He has homes in both London and Bali. Through Humanitad, Sacha is positioning himself as an "Interfaith Fighter for the World".

Unlike the organizations described earlier, Humanitad does not hold any routine events. Rather, it is focused on conducting artistic, cultural and educational programs to unify humankind.

Humanitad's current project in Ubud is the Earth Sanctuary. This ambitious project is described as a "blueprint for a new planetary model of sustainable and conscious living". The main focus of this project is the construction of a Temple of Humanity, which will function as a meeting place for the world's religious and spiritual leaders. The Temple of Humanity will also be a center for meditation, yoga and healing.

Another visionary project is the Monument to Mankind (M2M). It is not yet certain whether this project will be realized in Ubud or somewhere else. M2M is a project to build a gigantic four-sided pyramid with seven levels, adorned with a large sphere at its apex. Within the pyramid will be displayed specially commissioned art works by selected artists from 193 nations around the world.

Humanitad is clearly an organization with big ideas to unite global humankind. The spirit of this organization is wholly in line with the spirit of Ubud, with its emphasis on harmony and solidarity among people while respecting their differences.

Healing Treatment Centers

Apart from the international-scale organizations and events described above, another thing that has recently made Ubud more famous globally is the many healing treatment centers that have appeared in all parts of Ubud.

Healing treatment facilities can generally be categorized into two types: those that emphasize inner/spiritual health and healing, and those focused more on physical health and healing. The inner/spiritual healing treatment facilities include the yoga and meditation programs and centers described earlier.

The main facilities that emphasize physical healing treatments are spas. For guests at major hotels, spa facilities are taken for granted, and most of the hotels in Ubud have their own spa facilities.

The natural environment of Bali, and especially of Ubud, is ideally conducive to the development of spa facilities. In early 2009, Bali was declared "The Best Spa Tourism Destination in the World 2009" by *Senses* magazine, based in Berlin. The award was based on the choices of 60,000 readers and 200 spa experts from around the world.

The word *spa* derives from the name of a mineral water spring in Spa, Belgium, that has been known since the times of the Roman Empire (10th century BC to 5th century AD). The term "spa" now refers to any place that has a spring with healing properties. Essentially, spa treatment means healing through the use of water.[6]

Spa treatments have many benefits: enhancing physical beauty, improving physical fitness, and even healing ailments.

Interestingly, the spa treatments in Ubud do not simply copy those from outside Bali. Spa treatments here are combined with ancient Balinese healing rituals that have been passed down from generation to generation by the noble families in the *puri*. For this reason, spa treatments in Ubud use natural materials from in and around Ubud— roots, flowers, fruits, seeds, leaves, and other parts of plants. Ubud also happens to have hot springs that emerge from deep in the earth, with healing powers that can treat many ailments.

Spa treatments here are also performed with due respect to the community and the environment; facilities are closed off from public view and comply with the religious and traditional standards of Balinese society.

The most popular traditional Balinese spa treatments are Traditional Lulur and Traditional Boreh.[7] After these spa treatments, we are usually served traditional beverages—ginger drinks, or *jamu*, the healing herbal mixtures found throughout Indonesia.

One of the best known spa treatment facilities in Ubud is COMO Shambhala Estate at Begawan Giri. In 2009, this spa facility received the *Condé Nast Traveler* Readers' Spa Award in the World's Top 25 category, and in 2008 the Spa Asia Crystal Awards in the Best Complementary and Alternative Medicine Center category.

Other popular spa facilities in Ubud include Mango Tree Spa by L'Occitane at Hotel Kupu-Kupu Barong; Ayung Spa at Ubud Hanging Gardens; Kamandalu Spa at Kamandalu Resort and Spa; the Spa at Maya Ubud; Heaven & Earth Rejuvenation Spa at The Mansion; The Secret Garden in Desa Penestanan; and Bali Botanica Day Spa on Jalan Raya Sanggingan.

Tourists like to have their bodies pampered with spa treatments while they are in Ubud, and Ubud's environment is very conducive to this. As a result, spa facilities have become yet another of Ubud's many attractions. With this harmony between physical, mental and spiritual health and healing, Ubud has truly become a "global healing center".

Figure 8.5 Spa facilities in Ubud

Ketut Liyer: The Medicine Man

Ubud has recently become even better known to the outside world with the publication of the New York Times bestseller *Eat, Pray, Love: One Woman's Search for Everything* by Elizabeth Gilbert[8], which has sold over five million copies worldwide. There are plans to make the book into a film starring Julia Roberts and Javier Bardem.

As the title indicates, Gilbert relates her adventures during several months she spent sampling food in Rome, studying meditation at an ashram in India, and finally falling in love with a Brazilian named Felipe in Ubud. You can read the whole story for yourself if you buy the book.

Anyway, one of the central figures in the book is I Ketut Liyer. While she was in Ubud, Gilbert often sought personal advice from Ketut Liyer. Ketut Liyer has long been famous in Ubud as a healer and palm reader, treating both local people and tourists. In Hindu-Balinese society, such healers are called *balian*.

It's not certain exactly how old Ketut Liyer is, but the information below one of his paintings in Museum Puri Lukisan says that he was born in 1924.

The name Liyer means "clear light", and was given to him by his grandfather. Ketut Liyer is dark-skinned, missing many teeth, and has thinning white hair; as Gilbert says, he resembles Yoda in "Star Wars". He dresses very simply, wearing a Balinese headcloth (*udeng*), a T-shirt and a sarong.

Like most other Balinese, he's very friendly, has a good sense of humor, and enjoys telling people the story of his life. Ketut Liyer always refers to himself as "*kakek*" ("grandpa") when speaking to younger people, even if he has only just met them.

Ketut Liyer's home in Desa Pengosekan is very simple, like other traditional houses in rural Bali. There's nothing to indicate that he is known throughout the world; just a small sign saying "Ketut Liyer, Painter and Wood Carvings, Medicine Man".

Old *lontar* manuscripts and books are strewn about the house. He also has a number of paintings that he calls "magic paintings"—small pictures portraying the Hindu-Balinese gods. Ketut Liyer is famous as a painter; he considers Rudolf Bonnet his best mentor.

The main thing that makes Ketut Liyer's house different from his neighbors' is the many foreign tourists who come to visit him, especially since *Eat, Pray, Love* was published. Tourists queue up to have him read their palms.

Since he has so many foreign guests, Ketut Liyer tries to adapt by speaking in broken English, with an accent that is, frankly, very hard to understand. If a guest can't grasp what he's saying, usually a relative of his who happens to be around, or the tour guide who brought the guest there, will try to clarify.

When he reads a visitor's left palm, he always starts by saying that he is simply reading a palm, and whatever the results, it's best to trust in God. He then examines the lines on the visitor's hand, and sometimes also their back and feet.

From the lines on our hand, he can read our personal character, health, love life, and the overall course of our life, including how many lives we have had (the Hindu-Balinese believe in reincarnation). He can also detect whether we suffer from kidney or liver disease, rheumatism, or asthma, from his examination of our back and feet. At the end of the reading, he politely says, "That is what Grandpa knows; if it doesn't suit you, please do not be angry."

It's a truly unusual and unforgettable experience.

Ketut Liyer also enjoys having his picture taken with his guests. If you visit, be sure to take along your camera, get the picture printed at one of the many photo studios in Ubud, and give him a print. He always jokes that he looks so old and ugly, while the visitor in the picture with him looks so beautiful or handsome.

You can believe what Ketut Liyer tells you or not, but either way, it's very enjoyable. Meeting someone like Ketut Liyer is in itself a spiritual experience.

Figure 8.6 Ketut Liyer

Many other international events have been held in Ubud, for example the "Bali Deep 2008 Exhibition" from 9 November 2008 to 12 January 2009 at Museum Puri Lukisan.

This exhibition, with the slogan "Silence Your Mind and Learn to Listen to Your Heart", displayed the synergy between graphic art, painting, film, photography and music by artists from Japan—Keiko Mandera (Jero Wulandari), Koji Ikuta, Kyoko Kakehashi, Yuichiro Akao, Toshihisa Mafune, Yuji Yoshida, Zigen, Tatsuya Yoshihiro, QP, Yusuke

Okubo, and many others. Sixteen artists from Ubud and a group of students from Ubud State High School 1 also took part.

The various events, organizations and individuals discussed above are cultural ambassadors for Ubud. It is thanks to them that Ubud has become better known to the world.

And though they come from different countries, with different languages and cultures, foreign guests are accepted and welcomed by the community of Ubud. This shows once again that the Hindu-Balinese community of Ubud is able to accept differences as long as they do not conflict with the prevailing norms and values.

For the guests, the inspirations and lessons they receive while in Ubud are very valuable for them when the return to their respective countries. And conversely, for the people of Ubud, the friendships they enjoy with the guests are helpful as well; the people of Ubud learn more about the world's many cultures and can select suitable elements from them to serve as inspiration to develop Bali's culture.

In economic terms, the presence of all these visitors in Ubud obviously adds to the income of the local community, through hotels, transportation, food, arts performances and other activities. And the various festivals usually include fund raising events to support education, health, and family empowerment to further promote the community's welfare.

These events and organizations also show that Ubud is more than just a tourism destination; it has also become a center for the study of culture and discussions of global issues. Ubud is a very inspiring and spiritual place.

With these various world-class events and organizations, Ubud has become a part of the global community. Ubud can make significant contributions to solving the many problems that the world currently faces.

(Endnotes)

1 This story of the Ubud Writers & Readers Festival is taken primarily from the festival's website, http://www.ubudwritersfestival.com.

2 Explanations about *Skala-Niskala* and *Tri Hita Karana* can be seen in the preceding chapters. *Suka-Duka* (happiness and sorrow) is a philosophy of social solidarity that has survived for centuries in Hindu-Balinese society. Suka-Duka is the pillar of the banjar organization, whereby each member of the banjar is supported by all other banjar members both in joyous events such as weddings and in sad events such as deaths.

3 This story of the Quest for Global Healing Conferences and the Bali Institute for Global Renewal is taken from the websites of these two institutions, http://www.questforglobalhealing.org and http://www.baliinstitute.org.

4 This story of the Balispirit Festival comes mostly from the festival's website, http://www.balispiritfestival.com

5 This story about Humanitad is taken mostly from an interview with Sacha Adams Stone and from the organization's website, http://www.humanitad.org.

6 Others say that the word *spa* is an acronym of the Latin phrase "Salus Per Aquam" or "Sanitas Per Aquam", meaning "health through water", but this is a folk etymology that only emerged in the early 21st century, and therefore more properly considered a "backronym". The word or alleged "abbreviation" existed first, then someone tried to discover what it "stood for". Furthermore, the use of acronyms only became common in the 20th century; they did not exist as such in Roman times.

7 *Lulur* is an herbal skin scrub, followed by a refreshing yogurt massage for the skin, and finishing with a tropical flower bath and herbal "jamu" beverages for slimming or rejuvenation. *Boreh* is an ancient spice recipe of cloves, ginger, nutmeg and galangal root, designed to increase blood circulation. The mixture is lightly applied, then followed with a full acupressure body massage, complemented with a sandalwood moisturizer.

8 Elizabeth Gilbert, *Eat, Pray, Love: One Woman's Search for Everything across Italy, India and Indonesia,* Penguin, January 2007.

Chapter 9

Business with Values

"I'm always grateful if I can keep up with my social obligations while looking after my family's business."
Tjokorda Gde Raka Sukawati (Tjok 'De)

One interesting thing we can learn from Ubud is its business management. Business management in Ubud differs from business management in other places, mainly because Ubud's society still firmly upholds cultural and spiritual values that have been passed down from generation to generation. For this reason, business practices that are considered standard elsewhere could well be inappropriate if applied in Ubud.

As we explained in the Prologue, the best form of marketing—and marketing is the foundation of business—to enable a business to survive and prosper is to have business practices that successfully integrate marketing with positive values. This kind of marketing practice is concerned with broader aspects beyond mere short-term financial profits. This is also one of the characteristics of Marketing 3.0.

We have seen for ourselves that these practices, integrating marketing and values, are widely applied in Ubud. Therefore, in this chapter we will explore in greater detail how such practices are implemented, taking as our example the management of the hotels in the Pita Maha hotel group: the Hotel Tjampuhan, the Pita Maha, and the Royal Pita Maha.

The hotel industry is one sector of the tourism industry, along with the restaurant and trade sectors. As we all know, the tourism industry is the dominant business sector in Bali, and indeed the critical determinant for the health of Bali's economy. For this reason, this illustration from the hotel industry, along with the restaurant businesses previously discussed in Chapter 6, will give us some insight into business management philosophy and practices in Bali, and specifically in Ubud.

Also, the Pita Maha hotel group is owned by the royal family of Ubud—the house of Puri Ubud. So by studying the management of these hotels, we will also see how the Puri Ubud family play a role as protectors of the local culture and leaders of the community, as well as operators of a business.

In the following description, we will examine how the values of Ubud have been applied, from the initial construction of the hotels to how they are managed today. [1]

Hotel Construction Philosophy

These hotels have been built with a unique philosophy. It's fairly accurate to say that the way these hotels have been constructed is a manifestation of the personal vision of the Puri Ubud family—the founders and owners of the hotels—to provide accommodation facilities that truly express the character of Ubud to their guests. Consequently, the hotel construction has been done with more attention to comfort in the heart than to the pursuit of financial profit.

For just one example, the physical construction is always completed first before any marketing efforts begin. This is unlike many other property developers, who often start marketing their properties before they have even been built. For the Puri Ubud family, it just feels better if the hotel is built first, and then marketed. If we start thinking about marketing the hotel at certain rates too far in advance, the construction stage might never get finished.

In addition, the hotels have been built entirely through self-financing, with no debt or borrowing from banks. Basically, this allows the work that needs to be done to proceed without pressure. Working this way feels more relaxed, since the work is being done in accordance with our actual wishes. And the results will also be better. According to Tjok 'De, if a business is "forced," it won't be attractive.

Building these hotels was a great challenge, as they were all built on steeply sloping riverbanks, in terrain with dense forests. Yet all the hotels were built without blueprints, relying only on previous knowledge and experience gained mostly from designing and building temples.

You can imagine how difficult this must have been. Tremendous imagination and creativity and strong technical competence were needed to realize the hotel buildings as planned.

The building materials also come from the surrounding area. For example, when undergoing their five-month orientation period at the Royal Pita Maha, all employees were asked to gather stones from the Ayung River to build the lagoon in the hotel complex.

The interior, exterior, and facilities of the hotels were all built using measures set by the founders and the employees themselves: "If I were a guest here, what would I need, what would make me comfortable," and so on. Input from tourists was also welcome, and very seriously considered. The expectation was that these hotels would be true homes for their guests while they are in Ubud.

The Pita Maha hotel group was the pioneer among hotels built by local residents in Ubud. Back then, few people in Ubud were willing to open hotels with full facilities; such enterprises were usually only undertaken by foreign investors. And the hotels' location, right on the river banks, was another breakthrough later followed by other hotels in Ubud.

Figure 9.1 Construction of the Royal Pita Maha (courtesy of the Royal Pita Maha)

Figure 9.2 Tjok 'De with his staff during hotel construction (courtesy of the Royal Pita Maha)

Human Resources

Compared with most other hotels, probably the most unusual aspect of these hotels is their human resource management, especially at the Royal Pita Maha. The hotel's employees had almost no formal training in hotel management skills, since at least half of them were originally the workmen who built the hotel—people from the local community.

But this is what creates the hotel's differentiation. The friendly service from these employees is completely sincere and genuine. Recruiting employees from the start like this also gives them a real sense of belonging and sense of ownership in the hotel.

This sincere service is also acknowledged by the guests. Guests say that the natural friendliness they experience creates warmth in their hearts. In contrast, it's by no means certain that more "professional" hotel service would produce such a genuine sense of comfort, because when ingratiating smiles are based on ulterior motives, people can sense the lack of sincerity.

This recognition from the guests is in itself a powerful form of marketing communication. These guests will certainly tell their friends and colleagues about the wonderful experience they had at the hotel. This is what is called "horizontal marketing", where customers share information among themselves.[2]

The warm service from the employees seems to be a manifestation of meaning behind the Pita Maha hotel group's logo, a red hibiscus flower. The hibiscus is known as a flower that can blossom any time, anywhere. And the hotel's employees also want to provide the guests with "fragrance" and "beauty", just like a hibiscus, whatever the time and place.

The employees are also given the opportunity, and indeed strongly encouraged, to take part in all traditional religious ceremonies. In the conventional business context, this would be considered detrimental, because working hours are sacrificed. In fact, however, this privilege makes the employees work with even greater devotion.

This is also a reason why nearly all the employees of the Pita Maha hotel group come from the local community of Ubud, unlike many other hotels, which recruit professional employees from outside Ubud. Hiring local people empowers the local economy, while people from outside Ubud have a certain degree of difficulty appreciating the local cultural values.

Tjok 'De says that the hotels have three customers, in line with Tri Hita Karana philosophy: God, nature, and people. People here includes employees, the community, travel agents, and the guests who stay in the hotels. This is why the Pita Maha hotel group's management always addresses the interests of all these customers.

Differentiation in Hotel Management

Differentiation is an important element in the world of marketing. Differentiation enables people to distinguish between one product and another.

Furthermore, if the differentiation is truly intrinsic to the product and difficult to imitate, the differentiation becomes like the DNA in a person. Each person's DNA is unique and creates a clear differentiation between that individual and others.

Differentiation receives a great deal of attention in the management of the three hotels in the Pita Maha group. Broadly, the differentiation in these hotels can be categorized in two ways: differentiation in the hotels' physical aspects, and differentiation in the hotels' service and other non-physical aspects.

The differentiation in the physical aspect includes the hotels' locations on the banks of historic rivers, the layout adapted to these challenging sites, the design of the hotels in hand-made Balinese architectural style, and the use of local materials.

The differentiation in the non-physical aspect includes the genuinely friendly staff, employees who come from the local community with its banjar system, steeped in the principles of solidarity and togetherness, and the hotel management's sincere attention to all social/cultural activities that take place in the local community.

Below we describe each of these aspects of differentiation.

Differentiation in Physical Aspects

All three of the Pita Maha hotels have very historic locations. The Hotel Tjampuhan and the Pita Maha are on the banks of the River Oos, while the Royal Pita Maha is on the banks of the Ayung River. As explained in Chapter 2, both rivers have tremendous historic, cultural and spiritual significance for the Balinese.

In terms of their layout, the construction of the hotels was adapted to the conditions of the riverbanks. All planning and design was done directly in the field by looking at the geographical and topographical aspects of the terrain. The hotels were built without the use of any blueprints or master plans to guide the construction process or the architecture of the buildings.

Each hotel's layout is also arranged to include the river itself as an attraction. Every villa has a view of the river, and the elevations of the villas are arranged to avoid overlaps.

The third aspect of physical differentiation is the Balinese architectural style used in the hotel design, which incorporates plenty of traditional Balinese ornamentation and artwork, such as paintings and carvings. This concept gives the design a natural touch by balancing the spiritual, natural, and human aspects, in line with the spirit of Tri Hita Karana.

The next differentiation in the physical aspect is the use of local materials such as limestone. Use of building materials from factories or from outside Ubud is kept to a minimum. The use of local materials stimulates the local economy, thereby promoting better relations with the local community. And the use of local materials also reduces construction costs, enabling the hotels to be more competitive.

Differentiation in Intangible Aspects

The first form of differentiation in the non-physical aspects is the employees' genuinely friendly attitude. They serve hotel guests as they would serve guests in their own homes; the guests therefore feel comfortable and want to stay longer.

This kind of service to customers is a critical factor in a service industry such as a hotel. If the service provided is truly hard for competitors to imitate and truly unforgettable for the customers, it can be considered "branded customer service".[3]

The next form of differentiation is that the employees come from the local community, with its banjar system, steeped in values of solidarity and togetherness. The existence of close personal bonds both within and outside the workplace automatically produces better teamwork. Every employee is motivated to give the best possible service; each employee has a tremendous sense of ownership and a sense of responsibility to do one's best.

The third aspect of this intangible differentiation is the hotel management's deep involvement in the social/cultural activities of the local community. And the foundation of this differentiation is none other than Tri Hita Karana.

The manifestation of this differentiation is the active role played by the employees in social/cultural activities together with other members of the local community. In the context of relations between humankind and God, the hotels' management helps the community to build temples. In the context of relations between humans and nature, the management actively manages and creates a beautiful environment around the hotels. And in the context of relations between humans, the management tries to hire as many local people as possible, starting from the physical construction stage, so that they feel the hotel's presence brings them benefits.

Guests are often invited to watch the traditional religious ceremonies taking place near the hotel. As well as enjoying an unforgettable experience, the guests also feel more respected, as they are accepted by and even mingle with the local community.

All this differentiation ultimately creates a unique attraction for both guests and prospective guests. Hotel guests sense a spiritual vibration within themselves, arising from this differentiation based on Tri Hita

Karana. The guests also feel at one with everything in Ubud, as if Ubud is the home that they have always longed for.

Now let's look in more detail at each of the hotels in the Pita Maha hotel group: the Hotel Tjampuhan, the Pita Maha, and the Royal Pita Maha.

Hotel Tjampuhan

The Hotel Tjampuhan, built in 1928, was the first hotel in Ubud. Initially, this hotel was the home of Walter Spies. After his death, the building then used as a guest house. The hotel was later renovated and expanded, starting in 1986 and finished five years later. The name of the hotel, which is on Jalan Raya Sanggingan, comes from the hotel's location in the historic Tjampuhan area.

The hotel was formerly a guest house for visitors to Puri Ubud; its fame began with the founding of the Pita Maha artists' association. As mentioned above, the legendary painter Walter Spies once lived here. This fact is commemorated in a relief on a wall in the hotel's garden, which reads (in translation): "From 1930 to 11 May 1940, here lived Walter Spies, born in Moskou (*sic!*) 15 September 1895, died 1942."

The hotel, whose full name is the Hotel Tjampuhan Spa, employs an open architectural concept, with many villas spread out throughout the grounds. The traditional Balinese atmosphere here is intense. The roofs are made of woven grass fibers, and the roof frames from bamboo. The walls are adorned with traditional Balinese carvings and paintings. Most of the furniture, such as tables and chairs, is made from wood and rattan by Balinese craftsmen.

The building pillars are decorated with Balinese sarongs in black, white and red checkered patterns (in Balinese, *poleng*). These colors symbolize what is called, in Hindu-Balinese belief, the Trimurti. Red represents the god Dewa Brahma, the Creator; black is for Dewa Wisnu, the Preserver or Protector; and white symbolizes Dewa Siwa, the Destroyer and Reincarnator. In the corners of the hotel lobby are

Balinese statues, also adorned with sarongs, roses, and *canang* offerings, creating an intensely mystical, spiritual ambience.

The hotel's atmosphere is very refreshing. It stays cool in the daytime; the sun's rays do not beam directly in, as they are deflected by the dense, leafy tropical vegetation. Animals such as birds and squirrels run free within the complex, and from below we hear the burbling River Oos. Small lagoons with goldfish, floating lotuses, and small statues in the middle invite us to linger in the hotel's gardens.

It's very quiet in the evenings; all you can hear is the crickets and other nocturnal animals, performing their nightly symphony. The lighting in the hotel area is deliberately faint so that guests can better enjoy Ubud's magical/spiritual ambience.

The hotel has a two-story restaurant called the Terrace Restaurant. At breakfast time, the restaurant is full of guests enjoying the breakfast buffet, which includes items such as toast with honey, strawberry or pineapple jam, and cheese spread; fruit juices—melon, watermelon, and orange; coffee, tea and milk; and main dishes such as fried rice, fried noodles, and scrambled eggs. Next to the restaurant is a set of gamelan that guests are welcome to play when it's not in use.

The Hotel Tjampuhan has two outdoor swimming pools, one of which is fed with natural spring water. You'll see one or two guests swimming or lounging around the pool area reading novels. The hotel also has a movie house and a library, for film or book lovers.

One of the hotel's main attractions is its spa, sauna, and massage facilities, located right on the edge of the River Oos, in a small grotto with a pond inside. This grotto is decorated with traditional stone- and woodcarvings, and offers cold and warm water pools for soaking, as well as a sauna.

The grounds of the Hotel Tjampuhan are quite extensive. Because the hotel is set on the sloping banks of the River Oos, many of the paths through the grounds have stone steps. At each crossing, there's a wooden signboard giving directions to the various villas.

The hotel contains 67 villas, all made from natural materials in typical Balinese architectural style. The windows are quite large, to let in the sunlight; the local wisdom has created an eco-friendly architectural style.

Guests can use the hotel's shuttle car if they want to visit other places in Ubud. The route from the hotel goes to Museum Puri Lukisan, Puri Ubud, Pasar Ubud, the Monkey Forest, and back to the hotel. Shuttle cars are also provided at the other two hotels, the Pita Maha and the Royal Pita Maha.

Another attraction of the Hotel Tjampuhan is the Pura Gunung Lebah complex, directly opposite the hotel. Probably no other hotel in Bali is located so close to such a holy and historic structure. We can enter Pura Gunung Lebah by taking a trail and a small bridge over the River Oos.

Figure 9.3 Hotel Tjampuhan

Hotel Pita Maha

The Pita Maha is also located on Jalan Raya Sanggingan, on the banks of the River Oos. But unlike the Hotel Tjampuhan, this hotel, whose full name is the Pita Maha Resort and Spa, is a new complex, built in 1994 and officially opened in December 1995. The hotel was built in response to the increasing numbers of tourists visiting Ubud.

The atmosphere at this hotel is generally similar to that at the Hotel Tjampuhan, and it also employs traditional Balinese architecture. Unlike the Hotel Tjampuhan, the Pita Maha ensures a greater level of privacy, with each villa surrounded by an individual wall.

From the main road, this hotel is easy to recognize, because at the main gate there's a giant statue of Rahwana abducting Dewi Sinta. From the lobby and the two-story restaurant, we can enjoy views of a tropical forest full of coconut trees, banyans, palms, and ferns, and also rice fields.

Near the hotel lobby are two *bale bengong*. Here we can watch wood carvers producing animal statues—ducks, owls, komodos, dolphins, rabbits and frogs. There are also egg painters, putting designs on empty goose or ostrich eggs.

Still in the front area is the two-story restaurant. There's also a lounge with a more modern interior, which provides television and computers connected to the Internet.

The gardens are very neatly laid out. The main swimming pool, facing the banks of the River Oos, also has a small bar. Because of the hilly landscape, many of the garden paths have stone steps.

This hotel has 24 villas, all in traditional Balinese architectural style. Some villas have private gardens and swimming pools. The windows are wide; this not only conserves electricity but also gives a better view of the natural surroundings. Nevertheless, no one can see into your villa, because it's surrounded by a wall. The villas also have broadband Internet connections.

Each villa has a special space for relaxation. The shower and Jacuzzi are outdoors, but again, no one can see in, so guests can use these facilities in complete comfort.

The locks on the gates of the villas are unusual, consisting of wooden slide bolts and metal padlocks, rather than the electronic card locks now common in modern hotels. These traditional-style locks are consistent with the Balinese architecture. Even so, the villas are quite secure, since entry to the hotel complex is restricted to guests and hotel employees are constantly moving throughout the complex.

Unlike other hotels, the Pita Maha features a Private Villa Spa. This villa, open daily from 9 AM to 9 PM, offers spa treatments for physical beauty and health. Here guests can enjoy various types of massage, aromatherapy, and herbal treatments, normally for two hours. The villa can be used by individuals or in groups of up to five persons. This calm, relaxing open-air villa spa directly faces the River Oos.

Figure 9.4 Hotel Pita Maha

The Royal Pita Maha

The Royal Pita Maha is the Pita Maha hotel group's most premium hotel. While the other two hotels are on Jalan Raya Sanggingan, the Royal Pita Maha is on Jalan Raya Kedewatan, along the Ayung River.

The Royal Pita Maha—full name: The Royal Pita Maha: A Tjampuhan Relaxation Resort—was built starting in 1999. The hotel currently has 48 highly exclusive villas in Balinese architectural style. As demand is constantly growing, new villas are still being built; the plan is to have up to 100 villas within the complex.

The Royal Pita Maha, with the tagline "healing center", has very impressive facilities and views. It's on a very large plot of land—18 hectares—and set back a good 200 meters from the main road, up a private drive.

At the main entry are two large statues of *bidadari,* or nymphs. The view from the hotel's open-air, three-story restaurant is truly spectacular—a splendid panorama of the banks of the Ayung River, full of dense vegetation. The atmosphere in the evenings is surreal, as if we're in another world.

We can enjoy this splendid view while indulging in the restaurant's culinary delights. The menu is extensive and varied: Balinese dishes, Western food, and other international cuisines. You're likely to see guests using their laptops while enjoying their food or drinks.

Still near the restaurant area, we can see woodcarvers and egg painters at work, producing some very interesting souvenirs. You can order a wooden name board, which will be ready in just one day. There are also candle holders made from cloves, which emit a pleasant aroma when a candle is lit.

This hotel, like the others, is built on steep terrain next to a river. Because of the different elevations of different parts of the hotel, a special lift tower is provided. The hotel complex is enormous, just like the palace of a Balinese king in days of old.

The villas are also large and luxurious. Each villa has a main bedroom and two other spaces to the left and right. The space on the left is the bathroom, which includes shower and Jacuzzi facilities, while the area on the right has a television and a desk, with a mini-bar.

The bedroom faces the private swimming pool and the banks of the Ayung River. The bedroom windows are wide and can be slid open to let in the fresh air of Ubud. We can also refresh ourselves in the private swimming pool, with its clear, greenish-blue water.

Within the hotel complex is a soaking pool fed with natural mountain spring water, believed to have healing properties. Other bathing facilities include a lagoon that can be used for swimming, in addition to the main swimming pool and the private pools at each villa.

Because it is right at the edge of the Ayung River, we can also wade in the river, as long as we watch out for the swift current. From here, we can also get a splendid view of the virgin forest in this river valley, as if we have stepped back into the past. We also see and hear birds and other animals in the wild.

One of the most important features of the Royal Pita Maha is the holistic Balinese wellness facility, officially called "The Royal Healing and Wellness Centre". Here we can engage in yoga, meditation, and other therapies under the guidance of highly experienced, internationally certified instructors. The wellness treatments here combine traditional Balinese methods with those from other places. The yoga facility is one of the world's best places for yoga, with a highly spiritual atmosphere due to its location right on the edge of the Ayung River.

Also by the river is a restaurant that serves only organic food. Many of the ingredients come straight from an organic garden next to the restaurant. From this restaurant, we can watch people river rafting, and even hear their excited shouts—it's like having front row seats for this spectacle. This is certainly one of the best places in the world to enjoy a hotel breakfast!

The organic restaurant serves healthy, low-fat, high-fiber organic food. Nothing is fried or grilled; all the food is steamed, boiled, baked or broiled, and only high-quality cold-pressed organic olive or coconut oil is used.

The menu is highly varied: American, Continental, Indonesian, and Oriental. It's a perfect place to relax and enjoy food that is not just tasty but also healthy. Organic food is, of course, good for our own health, but it's also good for the health of the earth, because no chemicals are used to grow it. This is yet another example of how Tri Hita Karana is applied in the daily lives of the Hindu-Balinese.

The Royal Pita Maha offers complete facilities. The Royal Pita Maha also has a meeting room that can accommodate around 200 persons.

Figure 9.5 The Royal Pita Maha

Social Entrepreneurship

Hotel business management like that described above is an excellent example of what is known in contemporary business practice as "social entrepreneurship"[4]. The operators of the hotel—the family of Puri Ubud—do not measure their business performance solely in terms of monetary profits; they also consider the impact of their business on the local community and the surrounding environment.

Thus, long before the term "social entrepreneurship" was even coined, the Puri Ubud family was already applying the principles of social entrepreneurship in practice. The simple definition of a social entrepreneur is a person who understands economic, social and environmental problems and then uses entrepreneurial principles to establish and operate a business that can provide solutions to those problems.

As explained by John Elkington and Pamela Hartigan in their book *Power of Unreasonable People: How Social Entrepreneurs Create Markets that Change the World*, social entrepreneurs engage in unusual business practices that often strongly contrast with those commonly employed in the world of business. But these social entrepreneurs end up being more sustainable, because they are able to elicit a commitment from the broader community to run their businesses. The community feels that they are not simply objects, but rather active participants in the business.[5]

The business model of social entrepreneurship is "more-than-profit"; as well as earning a financial profit, the business also applies positive values in its business practices.

For example, returning to the management of the Pita Maha hotel group, every time a major traditional religious ceremony is about to be held in Ubud, the occupancy rates at these three hotels are always high. This indicates a strong correlation—though it might be hard to define precisely—between visitors' interest in staying at the Pita Maha hotels and the performance of the traditional religious ceremonies.

What is certain is that it's the feeling that makes guests want to stay at these hotels. This feeling—or as Tjok 'De describes it, vibrations—is also what gives Ubud its intense taksu.

We can also see how historic values survive and work in synergy with modern values. The hotels' historic values are combined with positive aspects of modern hotel management and construction, such as the use of elevators and an on-line reservation system.

So that's a quick look at the business practices employed by the Puri Ubud family. In purely physical terms, some other hotels might be more attractive. But because all aspects of the Pita Maha hotels' construction and management are fully in line with the Tri Hita Karana philosophy, those other hotels don't have the same taksu as the Pita Maha hotels.

From the marketing perspective, each of the hotels in the Pita Maha group has its own differentiation. The Hotel Tjampuhan has strong historic importance, complemented by the presence of Pura Gunung Lebah right across the river. The Pita Maha has villas with greater privacy, right on the banks of the River Oos. And the Royal Pita Maha has the Royal Healing & Wellness Centre by the banks of the Ayung River.

But essentially, all three hotels share the same character: a sanctuary, a calm place for contemplation, where we can restore our physical, mental and spiritual health. These hotels are unrivaled as places of holistic healing.

This is part of the taksu of Ubud: how it has "translated" the local culture into the worlds of business and social affairs. Ubud has succeeded in perfectly blending the very different worlds of business and of society. The business world, by nature materialistic, individualistic, and results-oriented, works in perfect synergy with the social world, characterized by mutual self-help, volunteerism, sincerity, and a human orientation.

This is a good example of Marketing 3.0, as the business practices that are employed truly position humans as both the actors and the main objective in doing business. The application of Marketing 3.0 will also help make any business more sustainable.

(Endnotes)

1   The story of the management of the three hotels in the Pita Maha hotel group is based primarily on interviews with Tjokorda Gde Raka Sukawati (Tjok 'De) and the thesis he wrote, entitled *Influence of Differentiation Strategy on Satisfaction of Customers at Pita Maha: A Tjampuhan Resort & Spa in Ubud,* for his Master's program in Management in the Postgraduate Program at Udayana University, Denpasar, in 2004.

2   "Horizontal marketing", whereby interaction occurs between customers, is one of the characteristics of the latest marketing concept called New Wave Marketing. "Vertical marketing", in contrast, is typical of conventional marketing, where the only communication is one way, from the producer to the customer.

3   The term "branded customer service" was introduced by Janelle Barlow and Paul Stewart in the book *Branded Customer Service: The New Competitive Edge* (Berrett-Koehler Publishers, September 2006).

4   The term "social entrepreneurship" began to emerge around the 1960s and became increasingly popular in the 1980s and 1990s. Among the institutions that have popularized social entrepreneurship are Grameen Bank, Ashoka, the Schwab Foundation for Social Entrepreneurship, and *BusinessWeek* magazine,

5   John Elkington and Pamela Hartigan, *Power of Unreasonable People: How Social Entrepreneurs Create Markets that Change the World,* Harvard Business School Press, February 2008.

Epilogue

Becoming a Sustainable Destination

"...Ubud, which became a tourism area earlier (than Sanur and Kuta), has still managed to preserve its natural beauty, culture, and social order."
Tjokorda Gde Agung Suyasa

The various aspects we have explored in this book show how Ubud has been able to develop and survive in changing times. The carefully-balanced blending of the values of centuries-old local wisdom with positive influences from outside has created Ubud's unique, original culture. The expressions of this culture continue to grow and expand, but its basic spirit remains eternal.

This concept provides a holistic approach to life in all its practices. Ubud not only teaches "back to nature", as is currently popular in the West, but also "back to God" and "back to society".

From the marketing perspective, this is a holistic marketing concept and practice that encompasses spiritual marketing, social marketing, and eco marketing. This concept and its practices are intrinsic to the daily life of the people of Ubud. The idea of "corporate social responsibility" (CSR) seems alien to people in Ubud, because CSR has been practiced for countless generations before the business and marketing worlds even heard of the term.

Guided by Tri Hita Karana, the people of Ubud effectively and sustainably put all this into practice. They have proven that the spiritual, humanitarian, and environmental aspects must all proceed together in harmony to help us achieve a better life. This Tri Hita Karana philosophy is what gives Ubud its strong taksu.

It is also this Tri Hita Karana spirit that could perhaps be adopted more widely, not only within Indonesia but throughout the world. And this is indeed possible, as this spirit is in fact universal and so it can be applied by any nation on earth. By applying this spirit, the global community can more quickly achieve the Millennium Development Goals (MDGs) set by the United Nations[1].

Now, let's briefly review the concepts of Tri Hita Karana, which include harmonious relations between humankind and God, between humans and nature, and among humans, and how these relate to the context of Ubud's contemporary development.[2]

Relations between Humans and God: *Parahyangan*

In Hindu-Balinese belief, the natural universe comprises two worlds: the physical world (*skala*) and the unseen, non-physical world (*niskala*). Humans have a responsibility to ensure that these two worlds run together in balance and harmony, through various traditional religious rituals.

From this understanding, we can see that Hindu-Balinese society is deeply religious and spiritual. In their lives, they do not simply pursue worldly, material goals; rather, they strive to devote themselves fully as creatures of Almighty God, Sang Hyang Widhi Wasa. This is why the Hindu-Balinese community in Ubud so often performs traditional religious ceremonies at the many temples.

It is this spiritual aspect that makes Ubud such a sanctuary for everyone who comes here. Ubud brings peace and healing to the spirits of humans, who may be fatigued by the many problems that beset them.

While in Ubud, we increasingly recognize that we are in fact spiritual beings in physical bodies. This is why people always base their actions not solely on logic and reason, but also on intuitive/emotional and spiritual considerations.

For example, people in Ubud feel it's inappropriate to worry too much about the expense involved in performing traditional religious ceremonies or other social activities. For them, it's a matter of the heart, not one of profit and loss.

In physical terms, Ubud has certainly changed a lot. But spiritually, Ubud is just the same, or possibly even better. The traditional religious ceremonies, for example, are much larger than before. Ubud's populace, now more heterogeneous because of all the newcomers, has become more aware of their duties and responsibilities.

As long as the people of Ubud remember God and the history of their ancestors, everything will continue to run smoothly. The natural environment will remind them if they take too much from it. And the people also recognize that their lives are not just for the present, but also for the future.

This is the spirit that needs to be upheld and strengthened by the various elements of society in Ubud. Damage to physical facilities can be repaired, but if spiritual values are disrupted, these are much more difficult to restore.

So the relationship between humans and God, as manifested in the community's religious life, is critical. The Hindu religion—the soul of Bali's culture—gives Hindu-Balinese society its strong essential character. As long as the community of Ubud remains devoted to its religious practices and beliefs, its culture, character and spirit will survive.

Relations between Humans and Nature: *Palemahan*

The natural world is a blessing from God the Creator. In this world, many other creatures live alongside humans, both in the physical world of *skala* and in the unseen world of *niskala*. Therefore, all activities that relate to management of the environment are always accompanied by traditional religious ceremonies to honor God and these other creatures.

For example, when building a house or other structure, traditional Balinese architects (*unagi*) have always been concerned with the environmental aspect. Here are a few specific illustrations of this:

Buildings in Bali are designed on a human scale appropriate to their users, both to provide ergonomic comfort and convenience for the occupants and to avoid wasteful use of materials or land. Before building a house, the unagi first measures the homeowner's arm span, the length of his fingers, shoulder breadth, leg length, and so on. Only then does he determine the width and height of house's doors, the size of the house pillars, the length and area of rooms, and so on, all based on the owner's scale and measurements.

To conserve energy, house windows are large, to let in plenty of natural light. Roofs are also high, to promote natural air circulation and keep the house cool without needing air conditioning. The building materials also provide a kind of natural insulation that absorbs cold or heat on the outside of the building so that the inside is neither too hot nor too cold.

Traditional Balinese houses normally have large gardens with many plants. These green spaces are still preserved, to absorb water, absorb carbon dioxide and produce oxygen, reduce solar radiation, and comfort the heart.

Therefore, the construction that is done never damages the environment, because it is always performed with due attention to the matters just mentioned. Thus, problems, such as environmental degradation or social discrepancies, that occur elsewhere can be avoided here.

This cultural context for construction needs to be maintained, especially in Ubud, to prevent the erection of buildings based solely on the amount of budget available or on the wishes of architects who do not understand Bali's culture.

Bali's generations-old local wisdom can provide further inspiration to the "green building" concept that is currently becoming popular worldwide. Perhaps without their builders' even realizing it, buildings in Bali already embody the principles of green building—frugal with electricity and water, plenty of green plants—which protect the environment and help reduce global warming.

This awareness of the environment is what gives the community of Ubud a high level of what Howard Gardner calls "naturalist intelligence". Naturalist intelligence relates to the ability to recognize and interact with animals and plants, and sensitivity in reading natural signs such as the weather and soil characteristics.[3] Thanks to this environmental and natural awareness, Ubud remains a pleasant place to stay.

Environmental and urban planning issues have recently received considerable attention from world leaders. For example, at the World Urban Forum (WUF) IV in 2008 in Nanjing, UN Secretary General Ban Ki-moon reminded the world that cities that are not properly planned and managed may threaten the quality of the our air and water and thereby damage the environment.

Bali has been host to a large international conference on a related topic, the UN Climate Change Conference held in December 2007. This two-week conference, attended by over 10,000 participants from more than 180 countries, produced the "Bali Road Map" containing several important decisions to protect the world's climate in the future.

In the business sector, a "green business strategy" also has a positive impact on a company's competitiveness, and on its bottom line. Many now recognize that such business strategies are no longer merely an option, but are in fact necessary to survival.

Daniel Goleman, for example, in his book *Ecological Intelligence*, says that humans need to recognize that they live in an interrelated world with limited natural resources. Humankind therefore needs to be greatly concerned with conserving the environment, simply because we have no other choice. Once the natural resources in a given location are depleted, this causes difficulties not just for the people living there but for all of humankind.

And Thomas Friedman, in his book *Hot, Flat, and Crowded*, recommends an action he calls "Code Green": an effort by the world community to collectively replace inefficient energy practices with new energy systems that are clean, efficient, and preserve the environment (clean energy, energy efficiency, and conservation).[4]

At the level of Bali itself, a number of modern environmental management efforts have been undertaken. Several hotels, for example, have obtained Green Globe 21 certification from EC3 Global, an international environmental organization. Another initiative, by the Bali Hotels Association (BHA) in cooperation with Yayasan Wisnu and other organizations, has produced the first eco-rating guide for hotels in Bali.

When humans respect nature, nature will in turn respect humankind. This mutual respect between humans and nature needs to be maintained—as has so long been done by the community of Ubud.

Relations among Humans: *Pawongan*

The people of Ubud are famous for their friendliness. They love chatting with others, even with people they've just met. They are also known for their spirit of *gotong-royong*—mutual self-help—in various aspects of life. Before acting, they carefully consider the impact of their actions on others. It's fair to say that for people in Ubud, their greatest asset is their friends, neighbors, colleagues, and other people in general, in line with the communal principles of Ubud's society.

The solidarity among the people of Ubud is evident everywhere. Just look at any traditional religious ceremony, or other community social activities: everyone participates voluntarily, and all look happy performing their respective tasks. They do these things willingly, never asking why, or what's in it for them.

This sincerity and devotion can also be seen in the art works produced by Bali's great artists in the past. These art works, including paintings, were anonymous. It was only after the arrival of outside influences (Western artists) that these art works had names affixed to them, and then only to honor the artists who had produced them.

Furthermore, just as in any community, there are some people in the society of Ubud who are materially better off than some others. But this situation does not create social problems, because those who are better off help out those who are not doing so well. Differences in social status also pose no obstacles to social solidarity among the residents of Ubud. Nobles, market traders, hotel owners and even farmers—all respect one another and socialize warmly.

Because of this harmonious atmosphere in community life, Ubud— and Bali in general—almost never experiences serious conflicts within the community, or between institutions (for example, between the government and non-governmental organizations). Nearly all problems that arise are resolved at the banjar level and therefore do not spread.

Bali's traditional infrastructure supports this communal lifestyle. Every home has a *bale dangin*—a place to perform ceremonies relating to the family members, such as the birth of a child, the tooth-filing ceremony, weddings, funerals and so on. And at the banjar level, each banjar has its *wantilan,* the place for meetings of all banjar members.

This kind of intensely communal life may seem odd to people from outside Ubud. And in the context of contemporary business, which strongly emphasizes individualism and material success, some people might ask whether this kind of communal life is still appropriate.

The answer is easy: Of course it is. The community of Ubud has proven this for centuries. In contrast, the modern business world often experiences shocks precisely because of people's individualism and greed.

Basically, people need to cooperate to survive and have a better life. In the contemporary business context, we have recently entered what is called "the Participation Age". With the support of technological developments—including the Internet and Web 2.0—participation and cooperation between people is increasingly easy and mutually advantageous.[5]

In his book *The Necessary Revolution*, Peter Senge, an intellectual at MIT's Sloan School of Management, discusses how collective efforts from many groups in society can produce better solutions for human life.[6]

The habits and attitudes of mutual self-help and sincere devotion in the community of Ubud eventually also "infect" tourists who visit Ubud. Quite a few of them end up deciding to live in Ubud. The native residents of Ubud and these newcomers jointly protect the harmony of life in Ubud.

With its Tri Hita Karana, Ubud has "given birth" to new people. Ubud is able to transform any person into a better person; altered not just in terms of outward behavior but also in terms of thought patterns and inner spirit.

In the context of marketing, Ubud is a destination known for its cultural uniqueness. Ubud's taksu is so intense that people easily fall in love with the place. This makes it relatively easy to market Ubud. The objective of these marketing efforts is, of course, to make life in Ubud even better.

Since the early days, efforts—in various forms—to market Ubud have not required very great expenditures. Ubud has a strong brand and character that make it easily recognizable. Also, efforts to market Ubud have been conducted not only by the government; other elements of society have played an equally important role. The efforts undertaken by the community on its own behalf show that the people of Ubud have a proud sense of belonging; for them, it's more than just a place to live or to do business.

What the people of Ubud do, in the context of "New Wave Marketing", is a type of *horizontal marketing* (marketing efforts that involve the community, making them more efficient), rather than *vertical marketing* (marketing efforts in the form of high-cost, one-way promotion).

Ubud also teaches the important lesson that the issues of spirituality, the environment, and human relationships are in fact indivisible. This differs from the Western perception that separates these three aspects; this attitude is part of the reason why processes and results are often not as expected.

The challenge for the future is how Ubud can continue to maintain this spirit in the face of increasingly rapid changes.

Tourism is Ubud's predominant business sector; it brings in income and provides employment for the whole community of Ubud. It's fair to say that Ubud's economy depends almost entirely on the tourism sector. Ubud—and Bali as a whole—has no other business sectors that can be relied on to support its economy, apart from tourism.

Data from Bank Indonesia indicate that the tourism sector plays the greatest role in supporting economic growth in the Province of Bali. Tourism, represented by the trade, hotel and restaurant sector, contributed over 28% to Bali's gross regional domestic product (GRDP) at the end of 2008, followed by the agriculture sector, which contributed just over 18% in the same period.

The performance of Bali's tourism sector in 2008 is indicated by the 1.9 million tourist visits to Bali, exceeding the government target of 1.7 million persons. Another indicator is the volume of foreign exchange transactions, which average around US$ 40,000 per day.[7]

The rapid growth of the tourism sector has spurred growth in its various supporting subsectors, such as hotels, restaurants, art shops, and recreational facilities, as well. More and more people from various backgrounds will visit or come and live in Bali, including Ubud.

All this needs to be considered very carefully, with attention to the cultural values and the environmental carrying capacity of Ubud. Policies for tourism sector development and the regional zoning plan must continue to refer to the Tri Hita Karana philosophy. The existing taksu of Ubud must not be disrupted through lack of prudence in anticipating present and future challenges.

Therefore, the paradigm that needs to be cultivated is one of "Developing Ubud", not "Development in Ubud". Only through this "Developing Ubud" paradigm can Ubud remain sustainable.

Ubud's success can inspire the rest of the world. Ubud, in line with the origin of its name, can provide *obat*, medicine—healing—for the many problems affecting the world today.

With its critical role in the development of Bali from the past to the present day, Ubud expresses the essential character of Bali. Ubud really is "The Spirit of Bali"…

(Endnotes)

1   The Millennium Development Goals, or MDGs, are eight targets set by the United Nations to address the issues of poverty and hunger, universal education, gender equality, child health, maternal health, HIV/AIDS, environmental sustainability, and global partnership. For more information, see http://www.un.org/millenniumgoals/

2   A more complete analysis of the application of Tri Hita Karana in the context of Bali's development can be read in the book Bali is Bali Forever: Sustainable in the Framework of Tri Hita Karana, published by the Tri Hita Karana Awards Team 2007 and edited by Berata Ashrama, I Gde Pitana, and Wayan Windia.

3   The term "naturalist intelligence" was introduced by Howard Gardner, a neuropsychologist at Harvard University, in 1999.

4   Daniel Goleman's views can be read in the book Ecological Intelligence: How Knowing the Hidden Impacts of What We Buy Can Change Everything (Broadway Business, April 2009), and those of Thomas Friedman in his book Hot, Flat, and Crowded: Why We Need a Green Revolution—and How It Can Renew America (Farrar, Straus and Giroux, September 2008).

5   The Participation Age is characterized by the existence of Wikimedia and Facebook, which enable people from all corners of the planet to interact and work collectively on projects.

6   For more on this, see the book The Necessary Revolution: How Individuals and Organizations Are Working Together to Create a Sustainable World by Peter Senge et al. (Doubleday Publishing, June 2008).

7   These data on tourism in Bali come from the Regional Economic Study for the Province of Bali, Quarter IV of 2008, issued by Bank Indonesia.

About the Authors

Hermawan Kartajaya

Hermawan Kartajaya is the founder and President of MarkPlus, Inc, a marketing professional services firm that he started in 1990.

Since 2002, he has also served as President of the World Marketing Association (WMA). The UK-based Chartered Institute of Marketing (CIM-UK) has acclaimed him as one of the "50 Gurus Who Have Shaped the Future of Marketing", the only Asian in the list apart from Kenichi Ohmae. Hermawan is also one of the founders of the Philip Kotler Center for ASEAN Marketing, together with Prof. Philip Kotler (Kellogg School of Management at Northwestern University, Illinois, United States) and Prof. Hooi Den Huan (Nanyang Business School, Singapore). Hermawan is also recipient of the Distinguished Global Leadership Award from the Pan-Pacific Business Association (2009).

Hermawan has written many books and articles, which have been published in Indonesia and abroad. He has written five books in collaboration with Prof. Philip Kotler: *Repositioning Asia: From Bubble to Sustainable Economy; Rethinking Marketing: Sustainable Marketing Enterprise in Asia* (also with Prof. Hooi Den Huan and Sandra Liu, Ph.D.); *Attracting Investors: A Marketing Approach to Finding Funds for Your Business* (also with S. David Young); *Think ASEAN: Rethinking Marketing towards ASEAN Community 2015* (also with Prof. Hooi Den Huan); and *Marketing 3.0: Values-Driven Marketing*.

As well as actively writing books, Hermawan is also regularly invited to speak at international forums in Asia, Europe and the United States.

Hermawan is the only Indonesian and also the only non-professor to have attended Harvard Business School's Executive Education Program (Program on Case Method and Participant-Centered Learning). He has also attended several other executive education programs conducted by the Wharton School of the University of Pennsylvania, Kellogg School of Management, University of Michigan Business School, INSEAD, and the University of Chicago.

Visit Hermawan Kartajaya's personal blog at www.hermawankartajaya. com, on Facebook (ID: Hermawan Kartajaya), and on Twitter (http:// twitter.com/hermawank).

Bembi Dwi Indrio M.

Bembi Dwi Indrio M. is a writer and researcher on business and marketing. Bembi is a graduate of the Bandung Institute of Technology (ITB).